Introduction to Commerce

Amit Vikram

Published by
ATLANTIC
PUBLISHERS & DISTRIBUTORS (P) LTD
7/22, Ansari Road, Darya Ganj,
New Delhi-110002
Phones : +91-11-40775252, 23273880, 23275880, 23280451
Fax : +91-11-23285873
Web : www.atlanticbooks.com
E-mail : orders@atlanticbooks.com

Branch Office
5, Nallathambi Street, Wallajah Road,
Chennai-600002
Phones : +91-44-64611085, 32413319
E-mail : chennai@atlanticbooks.com

Printed in India at Nice Printing Press, A-33/3A, Site-IV, Industrial Area, Sahibabad, Ghaziabad, U.P.

Preface

Building the foundations of even mega structures starts with the placement of the first set of blocks, also called "building blocks". The positions and strength of these initial blocks determine the stability and robustness of the entire structure. The better the blocks are placed, the higher the construction can be done on them. Rules for better and high quality education are no different from the rules of erecting mega structures.

The main objective of writing the book *Introduction to Commerce* is to provide simple and easy approach for understanding the basics of commerce and laying stepping stones for diligence. The book primarily covers six pertinent disciplines of commercial studies, namely Accounts, Economics, Human Resource, Statistics, Business Management, Concepts & Practices and Business Communication. It not only provides knowledge in a simple manner which is easily understandable, but also presents some useful and unique additional learning tips, wherever necessary, alongside conceptual material to enhance memorization of fundamentals. The book will immensely help fresh entrants in the field of commerce and provide them with insight to solve all sorts of problems pertaining to the discipline.

In short, the book has three uses:

- Understanding the basic concepts and fundamentals in an uncomplicated manner;
- Quick revision during examination time; and
- Ready reference.

Ideally, it should be used as a channel for initial understanding and must be supplemented by other literary works by renowned authors on the aforesaid disciplines, containing eloborate details for best results.

I sincerely thank my father, Dr. Rajendra Prasad (Associate Professor, Delhi University) who inspired me to write this book for addressing the problem areas pertaining to commercial subjects confronted by fresh entrants in commerce. This book is the result of his initiative and constant motivation. I am also thankful to my wife, Mrs. Anjali Vikram (corporate professional) for her constant support during my working on this book. Last but not least, I am grateful for the blessings and encouragement of my mother, Mrs. Malathi Prasad (Ex-teacher, Don Bosco School, Chennai), which paved the way for the completion of this book.

Finally, I would like to offer heartiest thanks to Atlantic Publishers and Distributors (P) Ltd. for publishing this book.

Amit Vikram

Contents

Introduction to Accounts

1

FINANCE AND ACCOUNTS

Essentials

The field of finance refers to the concepts of time, money and risk and how they are interrelated.

Accountancy: It is the system of recording, verifying, and reporting of the value of assets, liabilities, income, and expenses in the books of account.

1. **Financial Accounting:** It is a branch of accounting in which the financial information of business is recorded, classified, summarized, interpreted, and communicated; for public companies, this information is generally publicly-accessible (for external communication).

2. **Management Accounting:** Information is used within an organization and is normally confidential and accessible only to a small group, mostly decision-makers of that organization (for internal communication).

Financial Statements: Often referred to as books of accounts.

1. Balance Sheet: Referred to as statement of financial position or condition.
2. Income Statement: Referred to as Profit and Loss Account.
3. Cash Flows Statement: Reports on a company's cash flow activities, particularly its operating, investing and financing activities.
4. Statement of Retained Earnings: Explains the changes in a company's retained earnings over the reporting period.

Types	Purpose (in simple words)
Balance Sheet	Determines company's assets and liabilities structure along with owner's equity
Income Statement	Determines company's income, expenses, and profits over a period of time
Cash Flow Statement	Analyze the sources and uses of cash during an accounting period.
Statement of Retained Earnings	Tracks changes in a company's retained earnings over the reporting period

Generally Accepted Accounting Principles (GAAP)

- *Principle of regularity:* Consistency to enforced rules and laws.
- *Principle of consistency:* Application of the same methods and procedures from period to period.
- *Principle of sincerity:* Reflection in good faith the reality of the company's financial status.
- *Principle of the permanence of methods:* Allowing the coherence and comparison of the financial information published by the company.

- *Principle of non-compensation:* Portraying full details of the financial information and not seek to compensate a debt with an asset, revenue with an expense, etc.
- *Principle of prudence:* Showing the reality "as is". Typically, revenue should be recorded only when it is certain and a provision should be entered for an expense which is probable.
- *Principle of continuity:* An assumption that the business will not be interrupted.
- *Principle of periodicity:* Each accounting entry should be allocated to a given period, and split accordingly if it covers several periods.
- *Principle of full disclosure/materiality:* All information and values pertaining to the financial position of a business must be disclosed in the records.

UNDERSTANDING ACCOUNTS

Basic Accounting Equation

Assets = Liabilities + Owner's Equity (Owner's Investment)

What are Assets?

Everything of a value that is owned by a person, firm/business or company.

What are liabilities?

Any obligation of a person, firm/business or company.

What is Owner's Equity?

It is also called 'net worth' or 'shareholders' equity or 'net assets'. It is the owner's rights to the assets of the business.

Formula = Total Assets – Total Liabilities

Accounts are usually in "T" Format

Debit (Dr)	Credit (Cr)
Left Side is called Debit in Accounting	Right Side is called Credit in Accounting

What is Debit?

Debit has Latin roots. It comes from 'Debere', which means "To Owe".

What is Credit?

Credit also comes from the Latin word 'Credere', which means "To Hand Over".

DIFFERENT TYPES OF ACCOUNTS

At a Glance

Balance Sheet

Debit (Dr)	Credit (Cr)
Liabilities	Assets
Owner's Equity	*Land*
+ Net Profit	*Building*
– Net Loss	*Machinery*
Loan	*Cash*
Creditors	*Debtors*

They must always be equal. That's why it is a BALANCE SHEET.

Trading Account

Debit (Dr)	Credit (Cr)
Cost	Sales/Revenues
Raw Material Purchases	*Sales*
Wages to Laborers	
Gross Profit (If Income > Expenses)	*Gross Loss (If Income < Expenses)*

Income Statement (Profit & Loss Account)

Debit (Dr)	Credit (Cr)
Expenses	Income
Operating Expenses	*Gross Profit*
Salaries	*Interest Earned*
Overhead Expenses	
Net Profit (If Income > Expenses)	*Net Loss (If Income < Expenses)*

Expense Accounts

Debit (Dr)	Credit (Cr)
Opening Balance	
All Expenses Incurred (Increase)	*All Expense Decreases*
	Closing Balance

Income Accounts

Debit (Dr)	Credit (Cr)
	Opening Balance
All Income Decreases	*All Income Earned (Increasecs)*
Closing Balance	

Liability Accounts

Debit (Dr)	Credit (Cr)
Opening Balance	
All Liabilities Incurred (Increase)	*All Liability Decreases*
	Closing Balance

Asset Accounts

Debit (Dr)	Credit (Cr)
	Opening Balance
All Asset Decreases	*All Assets Acquired (Increases)*
Closing Balance	

☛ Tip to Learn

Basic Understanding

- Trading account is a part of income statement which depicts a firm's trading activities.
- Income statement, also called profit and loss statement (P&L), shows 'Net Profit' after deducting operating expenses from 'Gross Profit'.

Simple Rule

- Increase in assets and incomes are Debited, decrease is credited.
- Increase in expenses and liabilities are Credited, decrease is debited.

TRIAL BALANCE

Simple Example: Let us look at the accounts and finally the Trial Balance in the end.

Cash (Asset) Account* Remember the Rule

Dr (Increase in Cash) (Decrease in Cash) Cr

Description	Amount	Description	Amount
To Capital A/C	200,000	By Furniture A/C	20,000
To Goods A/C	12,000	By Rent A/C	5,000
	212,000		25,000
		By Balance c/d (Carried Down)	187,000
	212,000		212,000
To Balance b/d (Brought Down)	187,000		

- A worksheet listing balance of each ledger account in two columns, namely debit and credit, at a certain date.
- In a Trial Balance, the total of the debit side should always be equal to the total of the credit side.

Rent (Expense) Account* Remember the Rule

Dr (Increase in Cash) (Decrease in Cash) Cr

Description	Amount	Description	Amount
To Cash A/C	5,000		
	5,000		0
		By Balance c/d (Carried Down)	5,000
	5,000		5,000
To Balance b/d (Brought Down)	5,000		

Furniture (Asset) Account* Remember the Rule

Dr (Increase in Cash) | (Decrease in Cash) Cr

Description	Amount	Description	Amount
To Cash A/C	20,000		
	20,000		0
		By Balance c/d (Carried Down)	20,000
	20,000		20,000
To Balance b/d (Brought Down)	20,000		

Goods (Asset) Account* Remember the Rule

Dr (Increase in Cash) | (Decrease in Cash) Cr

Description	Amount	Description	Amount
		By Cash A/C	12,000
	0		12,000
To Balance c/d (Carried Down)	12,000		
	12,000		12,000
		By Balance b/d (Brought Down)	12,000

Capital (Liability) Account* Remember the rule

Dr (Increase in Cash) | (Decrease in Cash) Cr

Description	Amount	Description	Amount
		By Cash A/C	200,000
	0		200,000
To Balance c/d (Carried Down)	200,000		
	200,000		200,000
		By Balance b/d (Brought Down)	200,000

Trial Balance

Description	Dr	Cr
Cash A/C	187,000	
Goods A/C		12,000
Furniture A/C	20,000	
Rent A/C	5,000	
Capital A/C		200,000
	212,000	212,000

At a Glance

TRIALBALANCE

Account Title	L.F.	Debit Amount	Credit Amount
• Capital			√
• Land and Buildings		√	
• Plant and Machinery		√	
• Equipment		√	
• Furniture and Fixtures		√	
• Cash in Hand		√	
• Cash at Bank		√	
• Debtors		√	
• Bills Receivable		√	
• Stock of Raw Materials		√	
• Work in Progress		√	
• Stock of Finished Goods		√	
• Prepaid Insurance		√	
• Purchases		√	
• Carriage Inwards		√	
• Carriage Outwards		√	
• Sales			√
• Sales Return		√	
• Purchases Return			√
• Interest Paid		√	
• Commission/Discount Received			√
• Salaries		√	
• Long Term Loan			√
• Bills Payable			√
• Creditors			√
• Outstanding Salaries			√
• Outstanding Interest Earned		√	
• Advances from Customers			√

Contd.

• Drawings	√	
• Reserve Fund	√	√
• Provision for Doubtful Debts		√
TOTAL	XXX	XXX

Bank Reconciliation Statement

In a simple language: *A statement showing the items of differences between the 'Cash Book' balance and the 'Pass Book' balance.*

- **Cash Book:** *A subsidiary book which records the receipts and payment of cash.*
- **Pass Book:** *A book issued by bank to an accountholder. Its like a copy of the account of the customer in the books of bank.*

Cash Book and Pass Book are prepared separately. Individual, business concern or firm/ company prepares the Cash Book, while the Pass Book is prepared by the bank.

Both the books are related to one individual, business concern or firm/company and same transactions are recorded in both the books so the balances of both the books should match.

Ideally, Balance as per Pass Book = Balance as per Cash Book

When it does not happen, then it becomes necessary to resolve or reconcile the difference.

Causes of Difference

A transaction relating to bank has to be recorded in both the books (Cash Book and Pass Book). However, sometimes a bank transaction is recorded only in one book and not recorded simultaneously in other book. *This causes the difference at a given point.*

Causes	Cash Book Status	Pass Book Status
Balance as per	ABC	XYZ
Cheque issued by the company but not yet presented for payment	Decreased	Same
Cheques paid into the bank but not yet cleared	Increased	Same
Interest allowed/given by the bank	Same	Increased
Interest/expenses charged by the bank	Same	Decreased
Interest/dividends collected by bank	Same	Increased
Direct payments made by the bank	Same	Decreased
Direct payments received into the bank by a customer	Same	Increased
Dishonor of a bill discounted with the bank	Same	Decreased
Bills collected by the bank on behalf of the customer	Same	Increased
Errors committed either in Cash Back or Pass Book	**We need to check for Errors*	
We will arrive at	**PASS BOOK Balance**	**CASH BOOK Balance**

For reconciliation purpose, we can start with either *'Balance as per Cash Book'* or *we can start with 'Balance as per Pass Book'.*

- If we start with *'Balance as per Cash Book', then we will arrive at 'Balance as per Pass Book'.*

Simple Example

Causes	Transaction Status	Cash Book Adjustments	Required
Balance as per Cash Book		1,000	1,000
Cheque issued by the company but not yet presented for payment (500)	(500)	500	
Cheques paid into the bank but not yet cleared	200	200	(200)
Interest allowed/given by the bank	100		100
Interest/expenses charged by the bank	(400)		(400)
Interest/dividends collected by bank	300		300
Direct payments made by the bank	(700)		(700)
Direct payments received into the bank by a customer	600		600
Dishonor of a bill discounted with the bank	(200)		(200)
Bills collected by the bank on behalf of the customer	100		100
	700		1,100
		Cash Book Balance	We have arrived at Pass Book Balance

- If we start with *'Balance as per Pass Book', then we will arrive at 'Balance as per Cash Book'.*

Simple Example

Causes	Transaction Status	Cash Book Adjustments	Required
Balance as per Pass Book	1,100	1,100	
Cheque issued by the company but not yet presented for payment (500)	(500)		
Cheques paid into the bank but not yet cleared	200	200	
Interest allowed/given by the bank	100	100	(100)
Interest/expenses charged by the bank	(400)	(400)	400
Interest/dividends collected by bank	300	300	(300)
Direct payments made by the bank	(700)	(700)	700
Direct payments received into the bank by a customer	600	600	(600)
Dishonor of a bill discounted with the bank	(200)	(200)	200
Bills collected by the bank on behalf of the customer	100	100	(100)
		900	1,000
		Pass Book Balance	We have arrived at Cash Book Balance

Advantages of Bank Reconciliation Statement (BRS)

1. Helps in bringing out the errors committed either in Cash Book or Pass Book.
2. Shows any undue delay in the clearance of cheques.
3. Detects frauds by the entrepreneur's staff or bank staff.

Depreciation

In simple terms: *A non-cash expense that reduces the value of an asset as a result of wear and tear, age, or obsolescence.*

To be eligible for depreciation, an asset must have two features:

1. it has a useful life beyond the taxable year (essentially why it was capitalized in the first place), and
2. it wears out, decays, declines in value due to natural causes, or is subject to exhaustion or obsolescence.

Depreciation and Tax

When a company buys an asset that will last longer than one year, like a computer, car, or building, the company cannot immediately deduct the cost and enjoy an immediate large tax benefit.

Instead, the company must depreciate the cost over the useful life of the asset, taking a tax deduction for a part of the cost each year.

Important Points While Recording Depreciation

- For historical cost purposes, assets are recorded on the balance sheet at their original cost; which is also called the *historical cost.*
- Historical cost minus all depreciation expenses recognized on the asset since purchase is called the *book value.*
- *Salvage value* is the estimated value of the asset at the end of its useful life. It means once an asset is fully depreciated, no further expenses will be taken during its life.
- Because it is a non-cash expense, depreciation lowers the company's reported earnings while increasing free cash flow.

Methods of Depreciation

1. Straight-Line Depreciation
2. Declining-Balance Method
3. Activity Depreciation
4. Sum-of-Years' Digits Method
5. Units-of-Production Depreciation Method
6. Units of Time Depreciation
7. Group Depreciation Method
8. Composite Depreciation Method

Straight-Line Depreciation

$$\text{Annual Depreciation} = \frac{\text{Cost of Fixed Assets} - \text{Scrap Value}}{\text{Life of the Fixed Asset (Years)}}$$

Simple Illustration

- A vehicle depreciates over 5 years.

- Purchased at a cost of ₹ 17,000.
- Salvage value of ₹ 2000.

As per the formula above it will depreciate at ₹ 3,000 per year.

(₹ 17,000 – ₹ 2,000)/5 years = ₹ 3,000 annual straight-line depreciation expense.

Book Value at the Beginning of Year	Straight-Line Depreciation	Accumulated Depreciation	Book Value at the End of the Year
Original Cost			
17,000	3,000	3,000	14,000
14,000	3,000	6,000	11,000
11,000	3,000	9,000	8,000
8,000	3,000	12,000	5,000
5,000	3,000	15,000	2,000
			Scrap Value

Declining-Balance Method

Depreciation = Depreciation Rate × Book Value at Beginning of Year

Book Value = Original Cost – Accumulated Depreciation

Simple Illustration

- A vehicle depreciates over 5 years.
- Purchased at a cost of ₹ 1,000.
- Salvage value of ₹ 100.

Since the vehicle has 5 years useful life, the straight-line depreciation equals (100% / 5) = 20% per year.

With double declining-balance method, as the name suggests, double that rate, or 40% depreciation rate is used.

Book Value at the Beginning of Year	Rate	Depreciation	Accumulated Depreciation	Book Value at the End of the Year
Original Cost				
1,000	40%	400	400	600
600	40%	240	640	360
360	40%	144	784	216
216	40%	86.4	870.4	129.6
129.6	129.6 – 100	29.6	900	100
				Scrap Value

Activity Depreciation Method

Activity depreciation methods are not based on time, but on a level of activity. When the asset is acquired, its life is estimated in terms of this level of activity.

Simple Illustration

- A vehicle depreciates over 50,000 miles.

- Purchased at a cost of ₹ 17,000.
- Salvage value of ₹ 2000.

Hence, (17,000 – 2,000) / 50,000 miles = ₹ 0.30 per mile.

Sum-of-Years' Digits Method

Under this method, annual depreciation is determined by multiplying the depreciable cost by a schedule of fractions.

Simple Illustration

- A vehicle depreciates over 5 years.
- Purchased at a cost of ₹ 1,000.
- Salvage value of ₹ 100.

Steps in Calculation

1. First, determine years' digits. Since the asset has useful life of 5 years, the years' digits are: 5, 4, 3, 2, and 1.
2. Next, calculate the sum of the digits: 5 + 4 + 3 + 2 + 1 = 15.
3. Depreciation rates are as follows: 5/15 for the 1st year, 4/15 for the 2nd year, 3/15 for the 3rd year, 2/15 for the 4th year, and 1/15 for the 5th year.

Book Value at the Beginning of Year	Total Depreciable Cost	Rate	Depreciation	Accumulated Depreciation	Book Value at the End of the Year
₹ 1,000 (Original Cost)	900	5/15	300	300	700
700	900	4/15	240	540	460
460	900	3/15	180	720	280
280	900	2/15	120	840	160
160	900	1/15	60	900	**₹ 100 (Scrap Value)**

Units-of-Production Method

The useful life of the asset is expressed in terms of the total number of units expected to be produced.

Simple Illustration

- A vehicle depreciates over 6000 units.
- Purchased at a cost of ₹ 70,000.
- Salvage value of ₹ 10,000.

Steps in Calculation

1. A depreciable cost is computed.
   Depreciable Cost = Original Cost – Salvage Value.
   (₹ 70,000 – ₹ 10,000) = ₹ 60,000
2. Depreciation per unit is computed.
   Depreciation Per Unit = Depreciable Cost/Total Units of Production
   (₹ 60,000/6,000) = ₹ 10

3. Depreciation is computed.
   Depreciation Expense = Depreciation Per Unit × Units Produced during the Year.

Book Value at the Beginning of Year	Units	Depreciation Cost Per Unit	Depreciation	Accumulated Depreciation	Book Value at the End of the Year
₹ 70,000 (Original Cost)	1,000	10	10,000	10,000	60,000
60,000	1,100	10	11,000	21,000	49,000
49,000	1,200	10	12,000	33,000	37,000
37,000	1,300	10	13,000	46,000	24,000
24,000	1,400	10	14,000	60,000	**₹ 10,000 (Scrap Value)**

Group Depreciation Method

It is used for depreciating multiple-asset accounts using straight-line depreciation method. Assets must be similar in nature and have approximately the same useful lives.

Asset	Historical Cost	Salvage Value	Depreciable Cost	Life	Annual Depreciation
Car	17,000	2,000	15,000	5	3,000

Composite Depreciation Method

It is applied to a collection of assets that are not similar, and have different service lives. For example, computers and printers are not similar, but both are part of the office equipment.

Asset	Historical Cost	Salvage Value	Depreciable Cost	Life	Annual Depreciation
Computers	5,500	500	5,000	5	1,000
Printers	1,000	100	900	3	300
Total	6,500	600	5,900	5	1,300

- Composite life equals the total depreciable cost divided by the total depreciation per year. ₹ 5,900 / ₹ 1,300 = 4.5 years.
- Composite depreciation rate equals depreciation per year divided by total historical cost. ₹ 1,300 / ₹ 6,500 = 0.20 = 20%.
- Depreciation expense equals the composite depreciation rate times the balance in the asset account. (0.20 × ₹ 6,500) = ₹ 1,300.

Rectification of Errors

When a trial balance does not tally (that is, the totals of debit and credit columns are not equal), we know that at least one error has occurred.

The error (or errors) may have occurred at one of the stages in the accounting process:

- Totaling of subsidiary books.
- Posting of journal entries in the ledger.
- Calculating account balances.
- Carrying account balances to the trial balance.
- Totaling the trial balance columns.

It may be noted that the accounting accuracy is not ensured even if the totals of debit and credit balances are equal because some errors do not affect equality of debits and credits.

Classification of Errors

Keeping in view the nature of errors, they can be classified into the following four categories:

1. *Errors of Commission*: These are the errors which are committed due to wrong posting of transactions, wrong totaling or balancing of the accounts, wrong casting of the subsidiary books, or wrong recording of amount in the books of original entry, etc.

2. *Errors of Omission*: The errors of omission may be committed at the time of recording the transaction in the books of original entry or while posting to the ledger. These can be of two types:

- Error of complete omission
- Error of partial omission

3. *Errors of Principle*: Accounting entries are recorded as per the generally accepted accounting principles. If any of these principles are violated or ignored, errors resulting from such violation are known as errors of principle. An error of principle may occur due to incorrect classification of expenditure or receipt between capital and revenue.

4. *Compensating Errors*: When two or more errors are committed in such a way that the net effect of these errors on the debits and credits of accounts is nil, such errors are called compensating errors. Such errors do not affect the tallying of the trial balance.

Searching of Errors

If the trial balance does not tally, it is a clear indication that at least one error has occurred. The error(s) needs to be located and corrected before preparing the financial statements.

The following steps should be taken to detect and locate the errors:

- Recast the totals of debit and credit columns of the trial balance.
- Compare the account head/title and amount appearing in the trial balance, with that of the ledger to detect any difference in amount or omission of an account.
- Compare the trial balance of current year with that of the previous year to check additions and deletions of any accounts and also verify whether there is a large difference in amount, which is neither expected nor explained.
- Re-do and check the correctness of balances of individual accounts in the ledger.
- Re-check the correctness of the posting in accounts from the books of original entry.
- If the difference between the debit and credit columns is divisible by 2, there is a possibility that an amount equal to one-half of the difference may have been posted to the wrong side of another ledger account.
- The difference may also indicate a complete omission of a posting.
- If the difference is a multiple of 9 or divisible by 9, the mistake could be due to transposition of figures. For example, if a debit amount of ₹ 459 is posted as ₹ 954, the debit total in the trial balance will exceed the credit side by ₹ 495 (i.e. 954 – 459 = 495). This difference is divisible by 9.

Rectification of Errors

From the point of view of rectification, the errors may be classified into the following two categories:

1. *Errors which do not affect the trial balance.*

The rectification process essentially involves:

(a) Cancelling the effect of wrong debit or credit by reversing it.

(b) Restoring the effect of correct debit or credit.

For this purpose, we need to analyze the error in terms of its effect on the accounts involved which may be:

(a) Short debit or credit in an account; and/or

(b) Excess debit or credit in an account.

Therefore, rectification entry can be done by:

(a) Debiting the account with short debit or with excess credit,

(b) Crediting the account with excess debit or with short credit.

Simple Illustration

(i) Credit sales to Vikram ₹ 10,000 were not recorded in the sales book. This is an error of complete omission. Its affect is that Vikram's account has not been debited and Sales account has not been credited. Accordingly, recording usual entry for credit sales will rectify the error.

Vikram's A/c Dr. 10,000
To Sales A/c 10,000

(ii) Credit sales to Vikram ₹ 10,000 were recorded as ₹ 1,000 in the sales book. This is an error of commission. The effect of wrong recording is shown below:

Vikram's A/c Dr. 1,000
To Sales A/c 1,000

Correct effect should have been:

Vikram's A/c Dr. 10,000
To Sales A/c 10,000

Now that Vikram's account has to be given an additional debit of ₹ 9,000 and sales account has to be credited with additional amount of ₹ 9,000, rectification entry will be:

Vikram's A/c Dr. 9,000
To Sales A/c 9,000

2. *Errors which affect the trial balance.*

The errors which affect only one account can be rectified by giving an explanatory note in the account affected or by recording a journal entry with the help of the Suspense Account. In order to carry forwards the process of preparing the financial statements, the accountant tallies his trial balance by putting the difference on shorter side as 'suspense account'.

(i) Purchases book was under cast by ₹ 1,000. The effect of this entry is on purchases account (debit side) where the total of purchases is posted.

Purchase Account

Debit		Credit	
Description	**Amount**	**Description**	**Amount**
Under Casting Purchases Book for the month of...	1,000		
	1,000		

Simple Illustration

Trial balance of Anant Ram did not agree. It showed an excess credit of ₹ 16,000. He put the difference to suspense account. Subsequently, the following errors were located:

(a) Cash received from Amit ₹ 4,000 was posted to Ankit as ₹ 1,000.

(b) Cheque for ₹ 5,800 received from Anjali in full settlement of his account of ₹ 6,000, was dishonored. No entry was passed in the books on dishonor of the cheque.

(c) ₹ 800 received from Bhargava, whose account had previously been written off as bad, was credited to his account.

(d) Credit sales to Chanchal for ₹ 5,000 were recorded through the purchases book as ₹ 2,000.

(e) Purchases book under cast by ₹ 1,000.

(f) Repairs on machinery ₹ 1,600 wrongly debited to Machinery account as ₹ 1,000.

(g) Goods returned by Doli ₹ 3,000 were taken into stock. No entry was recorded in the books.

Solution

(a) Ankit's A/c Dr. 1,000
Suspense A/c Dr. 3,000
To Amit's A/c 4,000

(Cash received from Amit ₹ 4,000 wrongly posted to Ankit as ₹ 1,000, now rectified)

(b) Anjali's A/c Dr. 6,000
To Bank A/c 5,800
To Discount Allowed A/c 200

(Cheque received from Anjali for ₹ 5,800 in full settlement of his account of ₹ 6,000, dishonored but no entry made in books, now rectified)

(c) Bhargava's A/c Dr. 800
To Bad debts recovered A/c 800

(Bad debts recovered wrongly credited to Bhargava's account, now rectified)

(d) Chanchal's A/c Dr. 7,000
To Purchases A/c 2,000
To Sales A/c 5,000

(Credit sales to Chanchal ₹ 5,000 wrongly recorded through purchases book as ₹ 2,000, now rectified)

(e) Purchases A/c Dr. 1,000
To Suspense A/c 1,000
(Purchases book under cast by ₹ 1,000)

(f) Repairs A/c Dr. 1,600
To Machinery A/c 1,000
To Suspense A/c 600
(Repairs on machinery ₹ 1,600 wrongly debited to machinery account as ₹ 1,000, now rectified)

(g) Sales Return A/c Dr. 3,000
To Doli's A/c 3,000
(Sales return from Doli not recorded, now rectified)

Suspense Account

Debit		Credit	
Description	**Amount**	**Description**	**Amount**
Difference as per Trial Balance	16,000	Purchases	1,000
Amit	3,000	Repairs	600
		Balance c/d	17,400
	19,000		**19,000**

Note: Even after rectification of errors suspense account is showing a debit balance of ₹ 17,400. This is due to non-detection of errors affecting trial balance. Balance of suspense account will be carried forward to the next year and will be eliminated as and when all the remaining errors affecting trial balance are located.

Financial Statements

In simple terms: *They provide an overview of the financial condition, in both short- and long-term, about the financial affairs of a business organization.*

Financial Statements: Often referred to as books of accounts.

1. Balance Sheet: Referred to as statement of financial position or condition.
2. Income Statement: Referred to as Profit and Loss Account.
3. Cash Flows Statement: Reports on a company's cash flow activities, particularly its operating, investing and financing activities.
4. Statement of Retained Earnings: Explains the changes in a company's retained earnings over the reporting period.

Types	Purpose (in simple words)
Balance Sheet	Determines company's assets and liabilities structure along with owner's equity
Income Statement	Determines company's income, expenses, and profits over a period of time
Cash Flow Statement	Analyze the sources and uses of cash during an accounting period.
Statement of Retained Earnings	Tracks changes in a company's retained earnings over the reporting period

Balance Sheet

- Balance sheet is the snap shot of financial strength of any company at any point of time.
- Understanding balance sheet is very important because it gives an idea of the financial strength of the company at any given point of time.

Balance Sheet

LIABILITIES	ASSETS
Current Liabilities	**Current Assets**
Notes Payable	Cash
Accounts Payable	Petty Cash
Wages Payable	Temporary Investments
Interest Payable	Accounts Receivable - net
Taxes Payable	Inventory
Warranty Liability	Supplies
Unearned Revenues	Prepaid Insurance
Total Current Assets	
Long-term Liabilities	
Notes Payable	**Investments**
Bonds Payable	
	Property, Plant and Equipment
Total Liabilities	Land
	Land Improvements
Stockholders' Equity	Buildings
Common Stock	Equipment
Retained Earnings	Less: Accumulated Depreciation
Less: Treasury Stock	
	Intangible Assets
	Goodwill
	Trade Names
	Other Assets
Total Liabilities and Stockholders' Equity	**Total Assets**

Income Statement

1. Revenue: Revenue (or Sales) can be described as money earned from conducting the business's activities.

2. Expenses: Expenses are costs associated with business's activities. Generally, these are cash expenses. In addition, the income statement may include some non-cash expenses such as depreciation or amortization.

3. Net Income: The ultimate goal of any business is to produce a positive net income or profit over the long haul.

Line Items in an Income Statement

- **Net Sales** includes all sales reduced by any discounts or returns.
- **Cost of Goods Sold** includes all the costs of inventory sold, including production labor, materials, and overhead.
- **Gross Margin,** or Gross Profit is the first cut (Revenue – Cost of Goods Sold).

- **Operating Expenses** lists the total of expenses incurred to operate the business. Non-operating expenses such as interest expenses are excluded.
- **Advertising** includes any costs directly related to advertising products/services to potential customers.
- **Bad Debt** expense is used to write off invoices to customers who are not expected to pay.
- **Bank Charges** include any costs of banking for a checking account, merchant account, or other fees.
- **Depreciation and Amortization** is used to allocate the expense of fixed and intangible assets over a certain number of years.
- **Dues and Subscriptions** include costs of trade magazines or periodicals and membership dues to organizations.
- **Insurance** includes the cost of purchasing general liability or other insurance.
- **Licenses and Fees** include any costs incurred for occupational licenses, fees, or other licensing registrations.
- **Marketing and Promotion** includes any costs related to marketing to customers or helping establish the business's image.
- **Meals and Entertainment** includes the costs incurred for networking meals and other meetings with potential customers and advisers.
- **Miscellaneous** includes expenses that do not fit into any other category.
- **Office Expense** includes the expenses to run the office, including postage but not office supplies.
- **Office Supplies** includes the supplies you purchase for office needs, not including products that will be resold to customers.
- **Outside Services** includes money paid for outside consultants, sub-contractors, and other vendors.
- **Payroll**—Salaries, Taxes, and Benefits includes the entrepreneur's salary, benefits. Sole proprietors record their "salary" as an owner's draw.
- **Professional Fees** includes costs to hire a professional to help with different areas of a business such as management consultants, lawyers, accountants, etc.
- **Property Taxes** include taxes paid on the property owned by the business.
- **Rent** includes the specific costs of renting the business facility including common area maintenance costs, etc.
- **Repairs and Maintenance** includes all costs to maintain computers, equipment, and other capital purchases.
- **Shipping and Delivery** includes costs associated with shipping or delivering products/services.
- **Telephone** includes costs associated with local service, long distance, and mobile phone service, if applicable.

- **Training and Development** includes costs for employee training and development.
- **Travel** includes costs for traveling for business purposes to training sessions.
- **Utilities** include costs of utilities such as electricity, water, and gas.
- **Vehicle** includes actual costs incurred for company-owned vehicles or mileage reimbursement if the vehicle is not company-owned.
- **Leased Equipment** includes lease payments for equipment.
- **Operating Income**, also know as Earnings before Interest and Taxes (EBIT), is the income generated from conducting business.
- **Interest Expense** is the interest portion of the loan payments made during the year.
- **Other Income** is income received from activities other than the normal business operations such as non-operating rent income.
- **Income before Taxes** is a Net Profit calculation that is often used to compare one company against another since this figure has not been reduced by income taxes paid.
- **Income Taxes** are taxes levied by the government.
- **Net Income,** also known as Net Profit, is the earnings after taxes.

Income Statement

Expenses	Income
Cost of Goods Sold	Sales/Revenue (minus returns and allowances)
Gross Margin	
Operating Expenses	**Gross Margin**
Advertising	
Bad Debt Expense	
Bank Charges	
Depreciation and Amortization	
Dues and Subscriptions	
Insurance	
Licenses and Fees	
Marketing and Promotion	
Meals and Entertainment	
Miscellaneous	
Office Expense	
Office Supplies	
Outside Services	
Payroll Expenses	
Salaries and Wages	
Payroll Taxes	
Benefits	
Professional Fees	
Property Taxes	

Contd.

Rent	
Repairs and Maintenance	
Shipping and Delivery	
Telephone	
Training and Development	
Travel	
Utilities	
Vehicle (includes mileage)	
Leased Equipment	
Other	
Operating Income / Earning Before Interest and Tax (EBIT)	
	Operating Income / Earning Before Interest and Tax (EBIT)
Interest Expense	Interest Income
Income Before Tax (IBT)	Other Income (interest, royalties)
	Income Before Tax (IBT)
Income Taxes (if C Corp)	
Net Income	

Funds Flow Statement

In simple terms: *It is a statement which is prepared to disclose the changes in financial data of balance sheets of two periods.*

Objectives and Advantages

- Identification of sources (inflow) and utilization (outflow) of funds between two balance sheet dates.
- To know periodic increase or decrease in the working capital of a business.
- Helps in knowing the change in the financial structure of a business.
- It also acts as a process of budgeting.

Funds Flow Statement

Sources of Funds	Uses of Funds
Funds from Operations	Redemption of Shares
Issue of Shares	Repayment of Long-term Loans
Issue of Debenture	Purchases of Fixed Assets
Long-term Loan	Redemption of Redeemable Preference Shares Capital
Sales of Fixed Assets	Payment of Dividend
Non-Trading Income	
Decrease in Working Capital	Increase in Working Capital

Simple Illustration

Below are comparative Balance Sheets of a company say 'Synergy Limited' for two different years 1990 and 1991.

Liabilities			Assets		
Year	**1990**	**1991**	**Year**	**1990**	**1991**
Share Capital	1,000,000	1,100,000	Goodwill	50,000	40,000
Debentures	500,000	300,000	Land	420,000	660,000
General Reserve	200,000	200,000	Machinery	600,000	800,000
Profit and Loss A/C	110,000	190,000	Stock	250,000	210,000
Provision for Income Tax	40,000	110,000	Debtors (Good)	300,000	240,000
Creditors	50,000	40,000	Preliminary Expenses	30,000	20,000
Bill Payable	20,000	30,000	Cash	300,000	24,000
Provision for Doubtful Debt	30,000	24,000			
Total	1,950,000	1,994,000	Total	1,950,000	1,994,000

Additional Information:

(i) During the year 1991, a part of machine costing ₹ 7,500 (with accumulated depreciation ₹ 2,500) was sold for ₹ 3,000.

(ii) Income tax of 1990 was paid in 1991 ₹ 40,000. This is to be disclosed in the funds statement.

(iii) Depreciation on machinery for 1991 was provided at ₹ 50,000.

Now let us prepare a Statement of Change in Working Capital and a Statement of Funds Flow.

Solution

Statement of Change in Working Capital

Particulars	1990	1991	Change in Working Capital	
			Increase	*Decrease*
Current Assests				
– Stock	250,000	210,000	–	40,000
– Debtors	300,000	240,000	–	60,000
– Cash	300,000	24,000	–	276,000
			–	
			–	
Current Liabilities				
– Creditors	50,000	40,000	–	10,000
– Bills Payable	20,000	30,000	10,000	–
Working Capital	780,000	404,000	10,000	386,000
Net Decrease in Working Capital		(376,000)		

Adjusted Profit and Loss Account

To Provision for Income Tax	110,000	By Balance b/d	110,000
To Goodwill	10,000	By Provision for Doubtful Debts	6,000
To Depreciation	50,000		
To Loss on Sale of Machine	2,000		
To Preliminary Expenses	10,000		
To Balance c/d	190,000	By Funds from Operation (Bal. Figure)	256,000
	372,000		372,000

Machinery Account

To Balance b/d	600,000	By Cash - Sales	3,000
		By Profit & loss a/c - Loss	2,000
		By Depreciation	50,000
To Cash - Purchases	255,000	By Balance c/d	800,000
	855,000		855,000

Funds Flow Statement

Sources of Funds		*Uses of Funds*	
Provided by Funds from Operations	256,000	Land Purchased	240,000
Provided by Issue of Share Capital	100,000	Machinery Purchased	255,000
Provided by Sale of Machine	3,000	Redemption of Debentures	200,000
		Payment of Income Tax	40,000
Net Decrease in Working Capital	376,000		
	735,000		735,000

Cash Flow Statement

In simple terms: It is the summary of receipts and disbursements (or payments), reconciling the opening cash (and bank) balance with the closing balance of the concerned period with information about the various items appearing in the balance sheet and profit and loss account.

The Cash Flow Statement is partitioned into three segments—Cash flow resulting from:

1. *Operating Activities*
   - Receipts from the sale of goods or services.
   - Receipts for the sale of loans, debt or equity instruments in a trading portfolio.
   - Interest received on loans.
   - Dividends received on equity securities.
   - Payments to suppliers for goods and services.
   - Payments to employees or on behalf of employees.
   - Tax payments.
   - Interest payments.
   - Payments for the sale of loans, debt or equity instruments in a trading portfolio.
2. *Investing Activities*
   - Purchase of an asset.
   - Assets can be land, building, and equipment marketable securities.
   - Loans made to suppliers or customers.
3. *Financing Activities*
   - Proceeds from issuing shares.
   - Proceeds from issuing short-term or long-term debt.
   - Payments of dividends.

- Payments for repurchase of company shares.
- Repayment of debt principal, including capital leases.
- For non-profit organizations, receipts of donor-restricted cash that is limited to long-term purposes.
- Dividends paid.
- Sale or repurchase of the company's stock.
- Net borrowings.

Non-cash investing and financing activities are disclosed in footnotes to the financial statements.

Cash from Operations

Net Operating Profit

+ Decrease in Debtors and Bills Receivable
+ Decrease in Stock
+ Decrease in Prepaid Expenses
+ Decrease in Accrued Income
+ Increase in Creditors
+ Increase in Outstanding Expenses
+ Increase in Incomes and Advances
– Increase in Debtors and Bills Receivable
– Increase in Stock
– Increase in Prepaid Expenses
– Increase in Accrued Income
– Decrease in Creditors
– Decrease in Outstanding Expenses
– Decrease in Incomes and Advances

Net Operating Profit + Decrease in Current Assets and Increase in Current Liabilities – Increase in Current Assets and Decrease in Current Liabilities.

Cash Flow Statement

Cash Inflow	Cash Outflow
Opening Balance of Cash	Meet Business Losses
Issue of Share Capital	Purchase of Fixed Assets
Issue of Debentures	Purchase of Investments
Raising Loan	Repayment of Long-term Loans
Sale of Fixed Assets	Redemption of Preference Shares
Sale of Investments, etc.	Payment of Dividend, etc.
Other Miscellaneous Sources	**Closing Balance of Cash**

Below are comparative Balance Sheets of a company say 'Synergy Limited' for two different years 1990 and 1991

Liabilities			Assets		
Year	**1990**	**1991**	**Year**	**1990**	**1991**
Share Capital	300,000	400,000	Goodwill	115,000	90,000
10% Redeemabie Pref. Share	150,000	100,000	Land & Building	200,000	170,000
General Reserve	40,000	70,000	Plant	80,000	200,000
Profit & Loss A/C	30,000	48,000	Debtors	160,000	200,000
Proposed Dividend	42,000	50,000	Stock	77,000	109,000
Creditors	55,000	83,000	Bills Receivable	20,000	30,000
Bills Payable	20,000	16,000	Cash in Hand	15,000	10,000
Prevision for Taxation	40,000	50,000	Cash at Bank	10,000	8,000
Total	677,000	817,000	Total	677,000	817,000

Additional Information:

(i) Depreciation of ₹ 10,000 and ₹ 20,000 have been charged on plant account and land building account respectively in 1992.

(ii) An interim dividend of ₹ 20,000 has been paid in 1992.

(iii) Income Tax ₹ 35,000 was paid during the year in 1992.

Now let us prepare a statement Cash Flows.

Solution

Cash from Operations

Funds from Operation		218,000
Add: Increase in Current Liabilities (Creditors)	28,000	
Less: Increase in Current Assets		
– Debtors	(40,000)	
– Stock	(32,000)	
– Bills Receivable	(10,000)	
Less: Decrease in Current Liabilities		
– Bills Payable	(4,000)	
		(58,000)
	Cash from Operations	160,000

Cash Flow Statement

Cash Inflows		Cash Outflows	
Opening Cash in Hand and Bank	25,000	Purchase of Plant	130,000
Cash from Operation	160,300	Payment of final dividend for the last year	42,000
Sale of Land and Building	10,000	Payment of interim dividend	20,000
Issue of Shares	100,000	Payment of Tax	35,000
		Redemption of Preference Shares	50,000
		Closing Cash in Hand and Bank	18,000

Adjusted Profit & Loss Account

To Goodwill	25,000	By Balance b/d	30/300
To Depreciation-Plant	10,000	By Funds from Operation	213,000
To Depreciation-Building	20,000		
To Proposed Dividend	50,000		
To Interim Dividend	20,000		
To Prevision for Tax	45,000		
To General Reserve	30,000		
To Balance c/d	48,000		
	248,000		248,000

Plant Account

To Opening Balance	60,000	By Depreciation	10,000
To Cash Purchases (Balancing Figure)	130,000	By Closing Balance	200,000
	210,000		210,000

Building Account

To Opening Balance	200,000	By Depreciation	20,000
		By Closing Balance	170,000
		By Cash Sales	10,000
	200,000		200,000

Provision for Tax

To Cash-Tax Paid	35,000	By Opening Balance	40,000
To Closing Balance	50,000	By Profit & Loss a/c	45,000
	85,000		85,000

Financial Ratios

In simple terms: *They are mathematical relationship between one quantity and another.*

There are many categories of ratios such as those that evaluate a business entity's liquidity, solvency, return on investment, operating performance, asset utilization, and market measures.

Types of Financial Ratios

1. *Profitability Ratios:* Measure the firm's use of its assets and control of its expenses to generate an acceptable rate of return.
2. *Liquidity Ratios:* Measure of availability of cash to pay debt.
3. *Activity Ratios:* Measure how quickly a firm converts non-cash assets to cash assets.
4. *Debt Ratios:* Measure the firm's ability to repay long-term debt.
5. *Market Ratios:* Measure investor response to owning a company's stock and also the cost of issuing stock.

Sources of Data for Financial Ratios

The data is taken from the balance sheet, income statement, statement of cash flows or (sometimes) the statement of retained earnings.

Advantages of Ratio Analysis

- Useful in analysis of financial statements.
- Helps in simplifying accounting figures.
- Useful in judging the operating efficiency of business.
- Useful for locating weak spots of the business.

Disadvantages of Ratio Analysis

- They may give false results if based on incorrect accounting data.
- They cannot be compared if different firms follow different policies.
- They are highly dependent on price level changes.
- Results may be misleading in the absence of absolute data.
- They ignore qualitative factors.
- It is difficult to forecast future on the basis of past facts.

Abbreviations

- COGS = Cost of goods sold, or cost of sales
- EBIT = Earnings before interest and taxes
- EBITDA = Earnings before interest, taxes, depreciation, and amortization
- EPS = Earnings per share

Profitability Ratios

$$\text{Gross Margin} = \frac{\text{Net Sales} - \text{Cost of Goods Sold}}{\text{Net Sales}}$$

$$\text{Operating Margin} = \frac{\text{Operating Income}}{\text{Net Sales}}$$

$$\text{Profit Margin} = \frac{\text{Net Income}}{\text{Net Sales}}$$

$$\text{Return on Equity} = \frac{\text{Net Income}}{\text{Average Shareholder's Equity}}$$

$$\text{Return on Investment} = \frac{\text{Net Income}}{\text{Average Owner's Equity}}$$

$$\text{Return on Assets} = \frac{\text{Net Income}}{\text{Total Assets}}$$

$$\text{Return on Net Assets} = \frac{\text{Net Income}}{\text{Fixed Assets} + \text{Working Capital}}$$

$$\text{Return on Capital} = \frac{\text{Net Operating Profit} - \text{Adjusted Taxes}}{\text{Owner's Equity}}$$

$$\text{Return on Capital Employed} = \frac{\text{Net Income}}{\text{Capital Employed}}$$

$$\text{Return on Net Assets} = \frac{\text{Net Income}}{\text{Fixed Assets + Working Capital}}$$

$$\text{Efficiency Ratio} = \frac{\text{Non-interest Income}}{\text{Net Interest Income + Non-interest Income}}$$

Liquidity Ratios

$$\text{Current Ratio} = \frac{\text{Current Assets}}{\text{Current Liabilities}}$$

$$\text{Acid Test (Quick) Ratio} = \frac{\text{Current Assets – (Inventories + Prepayments)}}{\text{Current Liabilities}}$$

$$\text{Operation Cash Flow Ratio} = \frac{\text{Operation Cash Flow}}{\text{Total Debts}}$$

Activity Ratios

$$\text{Average Collection Period} = \frac{\text{Accounts Receivable}}{\text{Annual Credit Sales/365}}$$

$$\text{Degree of Operating Leverage} = \frac{\text{\% Change in Net Operating Income}}{\text{\% Change in Net Sales}}$$

$$\text{Average Payment Period} = \frac{\text{Accounts Receivable}}{\text{Annual Credit Purchases/365}}$$

$$\text{Asset Turnover} = \frac{\text{Net Sales}}{\text{Total Assets}}$$

$$\text{Inventory Turnover Ratio} = \frac{\text{Cost of Goods Sold}}{\text{Average Inventory}}$$

$$\text{Receivables Turnover Ratio} = \frac{\text{Net Credit Sales}}{\text{Average Net Receivables}}$$

$$\text{Inventory Conversion Ratio} = \frac{\text{365 Days}}{\text{Inventory Turnover}}$$

$$\text{Inventory Conversion Period} = \frac{\text{Inventory} \times \text{365 Days}}{\text{Cost of Goods Sold}}$$

$$\text{Receivables Conversion Period} = \frac{\text{Receivable} \times \text{365 Days}}{\text{Net Sales}}$$

$$\text{Payables Conversion Period} = \frac{\text{Purchases} \times \text{365 Days}}{\text{Accounts Payable}}$$

Debt Ratios

$$\text{Debt Ratio} = \frac{\text{Total Liabilities}}{\text{Total Assets}}$$

$$\text{Debt to Equity Ratio} = \frac{\text{Long-term Debt + Value for Leases}}{\text{Average Shareholders' Equity}}$$

$$\text{Long-term Debt to Equity} = \frac{\text{Long-term Debt}}{\text{Total Assets}}$$

$$\text{Times Interest-Earned Ratio} = \frac{\text{Earning Before Interest and Tax}}{\text{Annual Interest Expenses}}$$

$$\text{Debt Service Coverage Ratio} = \frac{\text{Net Operating Income}}{\text{Total Debt Service}}$$

Market Ratios

$$\text{Earnings per Share} = \frac{\text{Expected Earnings}}{\text{Number of Shares}}$$

$$\text{Payout Ratio} = \frac{\text{Dividends}}{\text{Earnings}}$$

$$\text{P/E Ratio} = \frac{\text{Market Price per Share}}{\text{Diluted EPS}}$$

$$\text{Cash Flow Ratio} = \frac{\text{Market Price per Share}}{\text{Present Value of Cash Flow per Share}}$$

$$\text{Price to Book Value Ratio} = \frac{\text{Market Price per Share}}{\text{Balance Sheet Price per Share}}$$

$$\text{Price/Sales Ratio} = \frac{\text{Market Price per Share}}{\text{Gross Sales}}$$

$$\text{PEG Ratio} = \frac{\text{Price per Earnings}}{\text{Annual EPS Growth}}$$

$$\text{EV/EBITDA} = \frac{\text{Enterprise Value}}{\text{EBITDA}}$$

$$\text{EV/Sales} = \frac{\text{Enterprise Value}}{\text{Net Sales}}$$

Cash Budget

In simple terms: *It is an estimation of the cash inflows and cash outflows of a business for future period of time.*

Characteristics

- It shows cash inflows and outflows.
- It monitors cash balances.
- It shows timing and amount of financing required.
- It usually has a short-term planning horizon.

Cash Budget Format

Particulars	Jan.	Feb.	Mar.
Opening Balance (A)			
Cash Receipts (B)			
+ Cash Sales			
+ Collection from Debtors			
+ Issue of Shares			
+ Raising Loans, Issue of Debentures			
+ Sale of Debentures			
+ Sale of Investments			
+ Sale of Old Fixed Assets			
Total of B			
Cash Payments (C)			
– Cash Purchase			
– Payments to Creditors			
– Payments of Expenses			
– Factory Expenses			
– Administration Expenses			
– Selling Expenses			
– Payment of Tax			
– Payment of Dividend			
– Redemption of Preference Shares			
– Redemption of Debentures			
– Repayment of Loans			
– Purchase of Fixed Assets			
– Purchase of Investments			
Total of C			
Closing Balance (D) = (A + B – C)			

Simple Illustration of Negative Cash Opening Balance

Information

Particulars	Feb.	Mar.	Apr.	May	Jun.
Sales	1,80,000	192,000	108,000	174,000	126,000
Purchases	124,800	144,000	243,000	246,000	268,000
Wages	12,000	14,000	11,000	10,000	15,000

Contd.

Additional Information:

(i) 50% of the credit sales are realized in the month following the sales and the remaining 50% in two equal monthly.

(ii) 25% sales are expected to be in cash.

(iii) Creditors are paid in the month following the month of purchase and 25% purchases are in cash.

(iv) Cash at Bank on 1st April = 10,000.

(v) Lag in payment of wages = one month.

Sales Calculation

Particulars	Feb.	Mar.	Apr.	May	Jun.
Total Sales	180,000	192,000	108,000	174,000	126,000
Cash Sales = 25% of Total Sales	27,000	43,500	31,500		
Credit Sales = 75% of Total Sales	135,000	144,000	81,000	130,500	94,500
Collection of 50% of the credit sales in the month following the sales	67,500	72,000	40,500	65,250	
Collection of the remaining 50% in two equal monthly installments	33,750	33,750			
Collection of the remaining 50% in two equal monthly installments	36,000	36,000			
Collection of the remaining 50% in two equal monthly installments	20,250				
Total Collection from Debtors			105,750	110,250	121,500

Purchase Calculation

Particulars	Feb.	Mar.	Apr.	May	Jun.
Total Purchases	124,800	144,000	243,000	246,000	268,000
Cash Purchases = 25% of Total Purchases	60,750	61,500	67,000		
Credit Purchases = 75% of Total Purchases	93,600	108,000	182,250	184,500	201,000
Payment to Creditors			108,000	182,250	184,500

Wage Calculation

Particulars	Feb.	Mar.	Apr.	May	Jun.
Wages to be paid	12,000	14,000	11,000	10,000	15,000
Wage Payment			14,000	11,000	10,000

Cash Budget

Particulars	Apr.	May	Jun.
Opening Balance (A)	10,000	(40,000)	(141,000)
Cash Receipts (B)			
Cash Sales	27,000	43,500	31,500
Collection from Debtors	105,750	110,250	121,500
Total of B	132,750	153,750	153,000

Contd.

Cash Payments (C)			
Purchases	60,750	61,500	67,000
Cash Payments to Creditors	108,000	182,250	184,500
Wage Payment	14,000	11,000	10,000
Total of C	182,750	254,750	261,500
Closing Balance (D) = (A + B – C)	(40,000)	(141,000)	(249,500)
Overdraft Required		(101,000)	(108,500)

Statement of Retained Earnings

In simple terms: *It is a financial statement, generated by a business concern, which shows the changes in retained earnings over a set period of time.*

Retained earnings are not paid out as dividends. Instead, they are retained and reinvested in the corporation. They are also called *earned surplus, retained capital,* or *accumulated earnings.*

Simple Illustration

Company ABC—Financial Information

Assets	250,000
Liabilities	70,000
Capital Stock	120,000
Retained Earnings	**?**

Solution

Assets = Liabilities + Capital Stock + Retained Earnings

As per the formula above we have 250,000 = 70,000 + 120,000 + Retained Earnings

Therefore, Retained Earnings = 250,000 – 120,000 – 70,000 = 60,000

Cost Accounting

In simple terms: *It is a branch of accounting dealing with the classification, recording, allocation, summarization and reporting of current and prospective costs and analyzing their behaviors.*

Cost accounting is frequently used to facilitate internal decision-making and provides tools with which management can appraise performance and control costs of doing business.

Various Managerial Accounting Approaches

- Standardized or Standard Cost Accounting
- Activity-based Costing
- Resource Consumption Accounting
- Throughput Accounting
- Marginal Costing/Cost-Volume-Profit Analysis

Classical Cost Elements

- Raw Materials
- Labor
- Indirect Expenses/Overhead

Purpose of Cost Accounting

- To establish cost methods and procedure that permit the control and if possible reduction or improvement of costs.
- To aid participating in the creation and execution of the plans and budgets.
- Creating inventory values for costing and pricing and described by law and at times controlling physical quantities.
- Determine company cost and profit for an annual or shorter accounting period in total or by segment as determined by management or required by government regulations.
- Providing management with cost information in connection with problems that involve a choice from among two or more alternative courses that is decision-making. The decision may be to enter a new market develop the cost for a new product discontinue a product line buy or lease equipment or take other action to decrease profits to solve problems.

Introduction to Economics

2

ECONOMICS

In simple words, it is the social science that studies the production, distribution, and consumption of goods and services.

The term economics comes from the Ancient Greek 'oikonomia', which means "management of a household, administration".

Classical Definition: A science of production and consumption of wealth.

Welfare Definition: A study of mankind in an ordinary business of life.

Scarcity Definition: A study of human behavior as a relationship between ends and scare means which have alternative uses.

Basic Problems of an Economy

Problems	Studies Under
What commodity shall be produced and in what quantity?	Price Theory
How to produce the goods?	Theory of Production
For whom to produce the goods?	Theory of Distribution
How to achieve the level of full employment?	Theory of Income and Employment
How to achieve efficiency in utilization of productive resources?	Welfare Economics
How to achieve maximum possible rate of economic growth?	Growth Economics

MICROECONOMICS

The study of economics at the level of individual consumers, groups of consumers, or firms. The general concern of microeconomics is the efficient allocation of scarce resources between alternative uses but more specifically it involves the determination of price through the optimizing behavior of economic agents, with consumers maximizing utility and firms maximizing profit.

–*Dictionary of Economics*

In simple terms: *It deals with economics decisions made at a low (micro), or individual level. Microeconomic theory is also called 'Price Theory'.*

Microeconomics looks at interactions through individual markets, given scarcity and government regulation. The theory considers aggregates of quantity demanded by buyers and quantity supplied by sellers at each possible price per unit.

Market structures such as perfect competition and monopoly are examined as to implications for behavior and economic efficiency.

In microeconomics, production is the conversion of inputs into outputs. It is an economic process that uses resources (manufacturing, warehousing, shipping, and packaging), to create a commodity that is suitable for exchange.

Factors of Production

- Raw materials
- Machinery
- Labour services
- Capital goods
- Land
- Enterprise

Economic Efficiency

Economic efficiency describes how well a system generates the maximum desired output with a given set of inputs. Efficiency is improved if more output is generated without changing inputs.

Pareto Efficiency *(named after Vilfredo Pareto, an Italian economist)*

Given a set of alternative allocations of goods or income for a set of individuals, a change from one allocation to another that can make at least one individual better off without making any other individual worse off is called a *Pareto improvement.*

An allocation when a change cannot make someone better off without making someone else worse off is called *Pareto efficient* or *Pareto optimal.* It is often called *strong Pareto optimum (SPO).*

Comparative Advantage and Absolute Advantage

Specialization is considered key to economic efficiency because different individuals or countries have different comparative advantages.

While one country may have an absolute advantage in every area over other countries, it could nonetheless specialize in the area which it has a relative comparative advantage, and thereby gain from trading with countries which have no absolute advantages. For example, a country may specialize in the production of high-tech knowledge products, as developed countries do, and trade with developing nations for goods produced in factories, where labor is cheap and plentiful.

Production Possibility Curve (PPC)

It is a curve that depicts the maximum level of production of specific goods and services that can be attained by an economy with given productive resources and techniques available. PPC only connects efficient production combinations.

Let us assume that the economy produces only two goods (watch and rice). Now, a country can either produce more of watch or of rice. Here, there can be many combinations of production.

- Maximum production of watch by employing all resources = OW

- Maximum production of rice by employing all resources = OR
- All possible points on the *WR curve* are *efficient levels of production*, e.g. E1 and E2.
- All points under (within) the *WR curve* are *inefficient levels of production.*

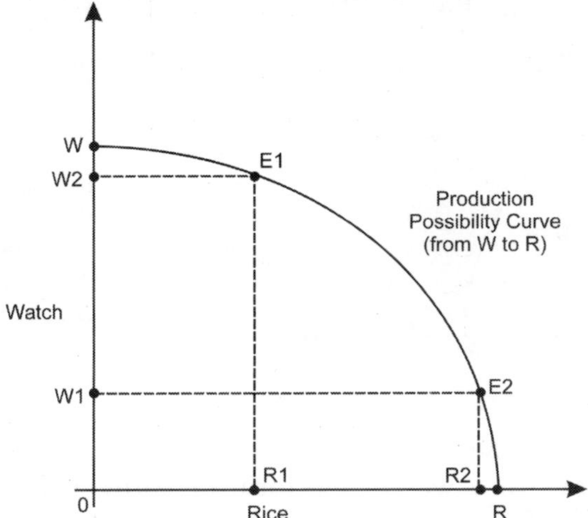

- All possible points on the *WR curve* are *efficient levels of production.*
- All possible points on the *W1R1 curve* are *inefficient levels of production.*
- Underutilization is the area between the two curves.
- An economy must try to find a way to utilize the resources to the maximum in order to life the PP curve to the ideal situation.

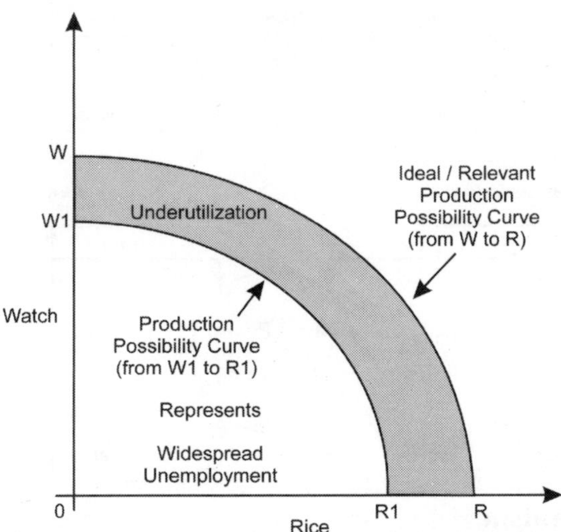

- A developing economy shows growth during a period (Upward shift of the PP curve from W1R1 to WR).
- A stagnant economy would remain at the same level.

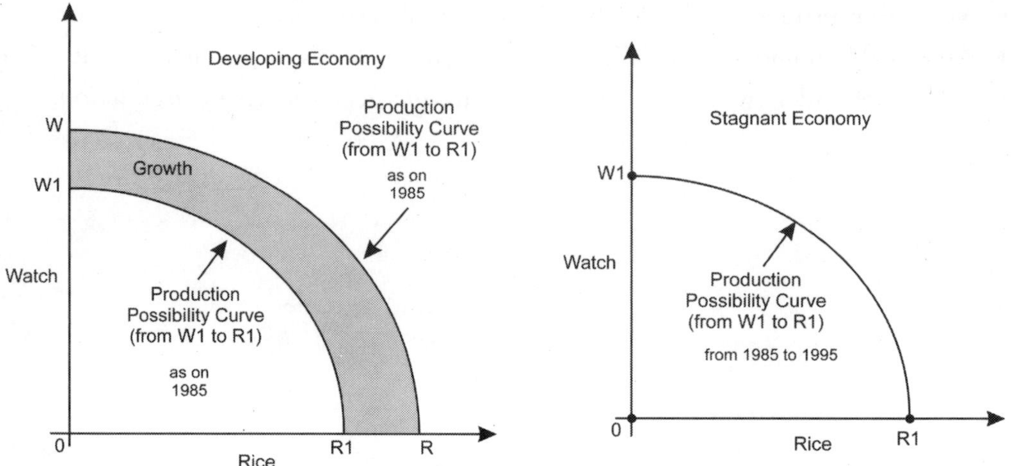

Price Mechanism

During the ancient era, trade was in the form of barter (exchange of goods with other goods). With the invention of money, a common measure for valuation of goods and services came into existence. This gave rise to price mechanism.

Working of Price Mechanism

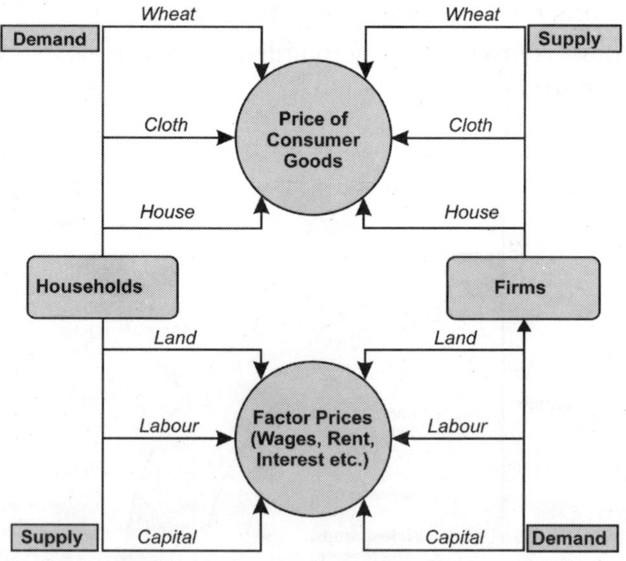

Issues with Price Mechanism

It works efficiently only when there is perfect competition among buyers and sellers. In the real world, many other forms of market exist, e.g. monopoly, imperfect competition.

Demand

Demand for a commodity is the desire to purchase that commodity by willingness to spend sufficiently available money for its acquisition.

Demand for a commodity at a given price is the amount of it which will be bought per unit of time at that price.

Demand Function

$D_n = f\,(p_n; p_1, p_2, p_3, p_4, p_5, p_6; Y, T, E)$

where

D_n = Demand for Commodity '*n*'.

p_n = Price of Commodity '*n*'.

$p_1, p_2, p_3, p_4, p_5, p_6$ = Price of related commodities

Y = Income of the Consumer

T = Taste of the Consumer

E = Expectations about Future

Law of Demand

All other factors remaining constant, as the price of a good or service increases, consumer demand for the good or service will decrease and vice versa.

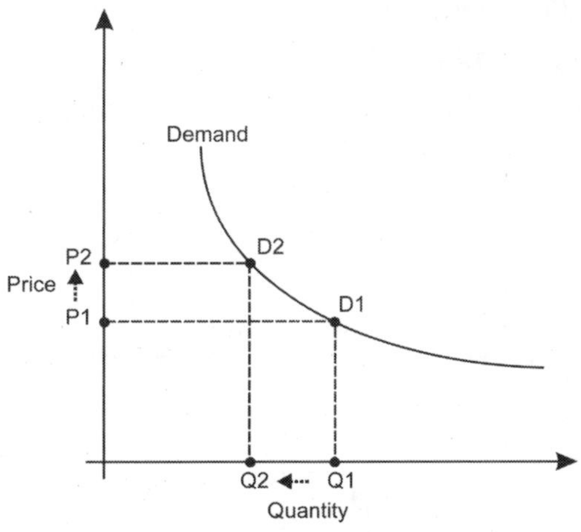

Price Elasticity of Demand

The measure of responsiveness in the quantity demanded for a commodity as a result of change in the price of the same commodity.

In simple terms: *Percentage change in quantity demanded as per the percentage change in price of the same commodity.*

$$\text{Price Elasticity of Demand} = \frac{\%\ \text{Change in Quantity Demanded}}{\%\ \text{Change in Price}}$$

$$\text{Price Elasticity of Demand} = \frac{\dfrac{\text{Change in Quantity}}{\text{Quantity}}}{\dfrac{\text{Change in Price}}{\text{Price}}}$$

Factors Determine the Elasticity

1. *Availability of Substitutes*: The more substitutes, the higher the elasticity, as people can easily switch from one good to another in case of even minor price changes.

2. *Nature of Goods (Degree of Necessity)*: The more necessary a good is, the lower the elasticity, as people will attempt to buy it no matter whatever is the price, e.g. insulin for those who need it.

3. *Different Uses of Goods*: The more a commodity can be put to different uses, the more will be the elasticity. With price rise, the consumers will buy goods with important uses.

4. *Percentage of Income*: The higher the percentage that the product's price is of the consumer's income, the higher the elasticity.

5. *Duration*: The longer a price change holds, the higher the elasticity, as more and more people will stop demanding the goods.

6. *Existence of Joint Demand*: In this case, the elasticity of demand of goods more important determines the elasticity of the other goods, e.g. ink and fountain pens.

7. *Fashion Taste and Preferences*: It depends from person to person.

Degrees of Price Elasticity of Demand

- *Perfectly Elastic:* Demand changes even without change in price.

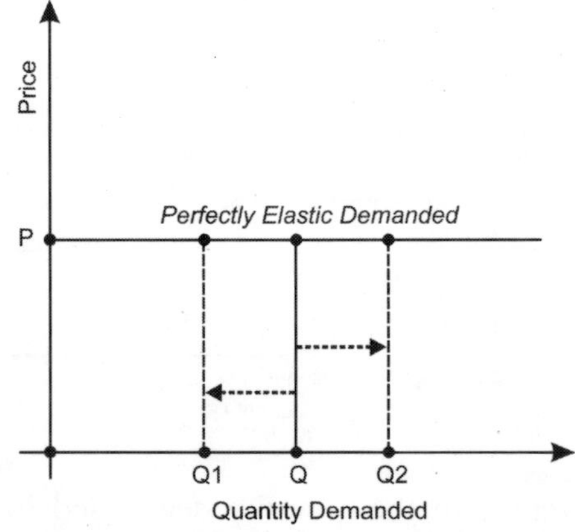

- *Perfectly Inelastic*: Demand never changes with change in price.

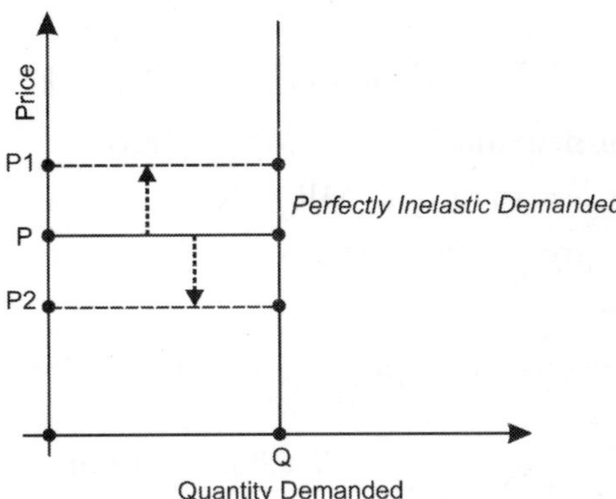

- *Unitary Elastic*: Percentage change in demand equals percentage change in price.
- *Elastic*: Percentage change in demand is greater than percentage change in price.
- *Inelastic*: Percentage change in demand is less than percentage change in price.

Price
P
P1
Unitary Elastic Demanded
Q1 Q
Quantity Demanded

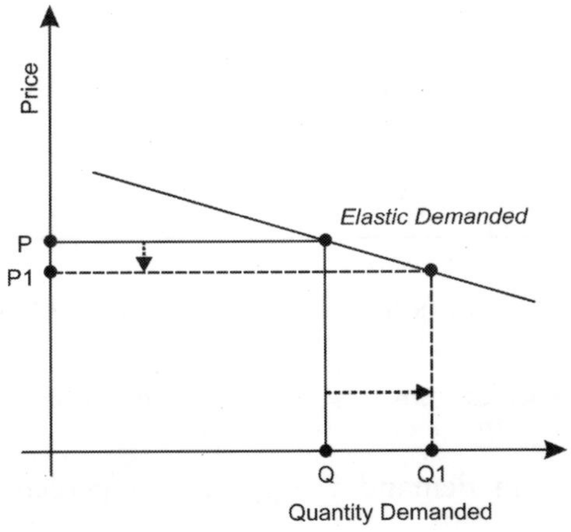

Price
P
P1
Elastic Demanded
Q Q1
Quantity Demanded

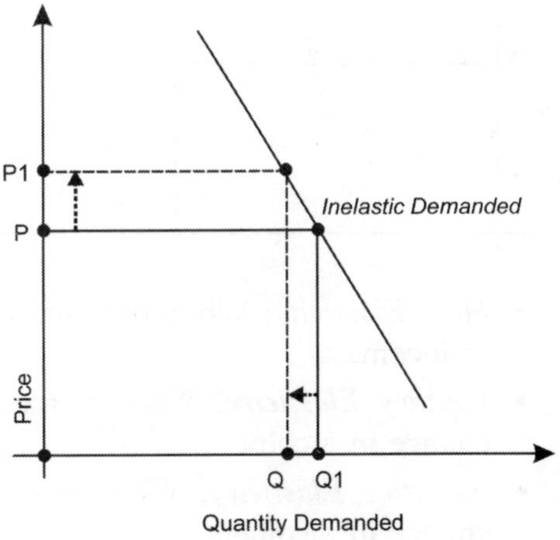

P1
P
Inelastic Demanded
Price
Q Q1
Quantity Demanded

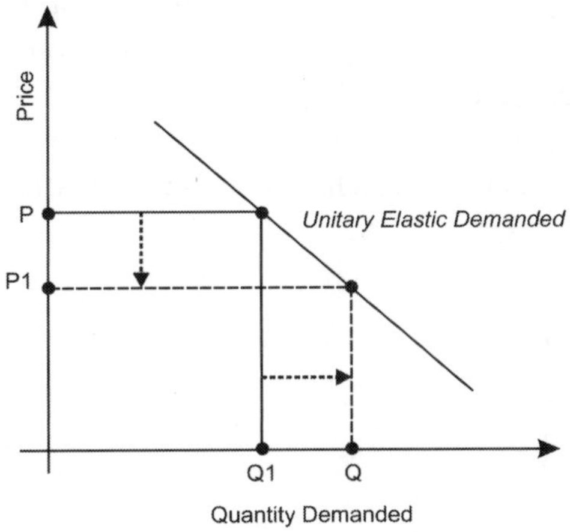

Relationship between Elasticity of Demand, Marginal Revenue and Average Revenue

$$\text{Price Elasticity of Demand} = \frac{\text{Average Revenue (AR)}}{\text{Average Revenue (AR)} - \text{Marginal Revenue (MR)}}$$

- When the elasticity of demand is unity, MR = Zero
- When the elasticity is less than one, MR = Negative
- When the elasticity is greater than one, MR = Negative

Income Elasticity of Demand

The degree of responsiveness in the quantity demanded for a commodity as a result of change in income.

$$\text{Income Elasticity of Demand} = \frac{\text{\% Change in Quantity Demanded}}{\text{\% Change in Income}}$$

$$\text{Income Elasticity of Demand} = \frac{\dfrac{\text{Change in Quantity}}{\text{Quantity}}}{\dfrac{\text{Change in Income}}{\text{Income}}}$$

- *Zero Elasticity*: When percentage change in demand is nil at any percentage change in income.
- *Low Elasticity*: When percentage change in demand is less than percentage change in income.

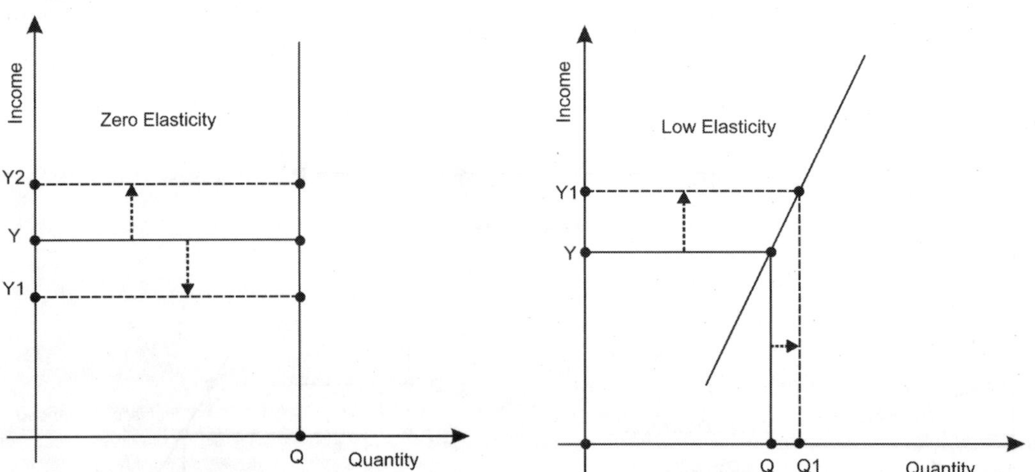

- *High Elasticity*: When percentage change in demand is larger than percentage change in income.
- *Unitary Elasticity*: When percentage change in demand is the same as percentage change in income.
- *Negative Elasticity*: When percentage change in demand is opposite to percentage change in income.
    - Income rises, demand falls (*e.g. Inferior Goods*)

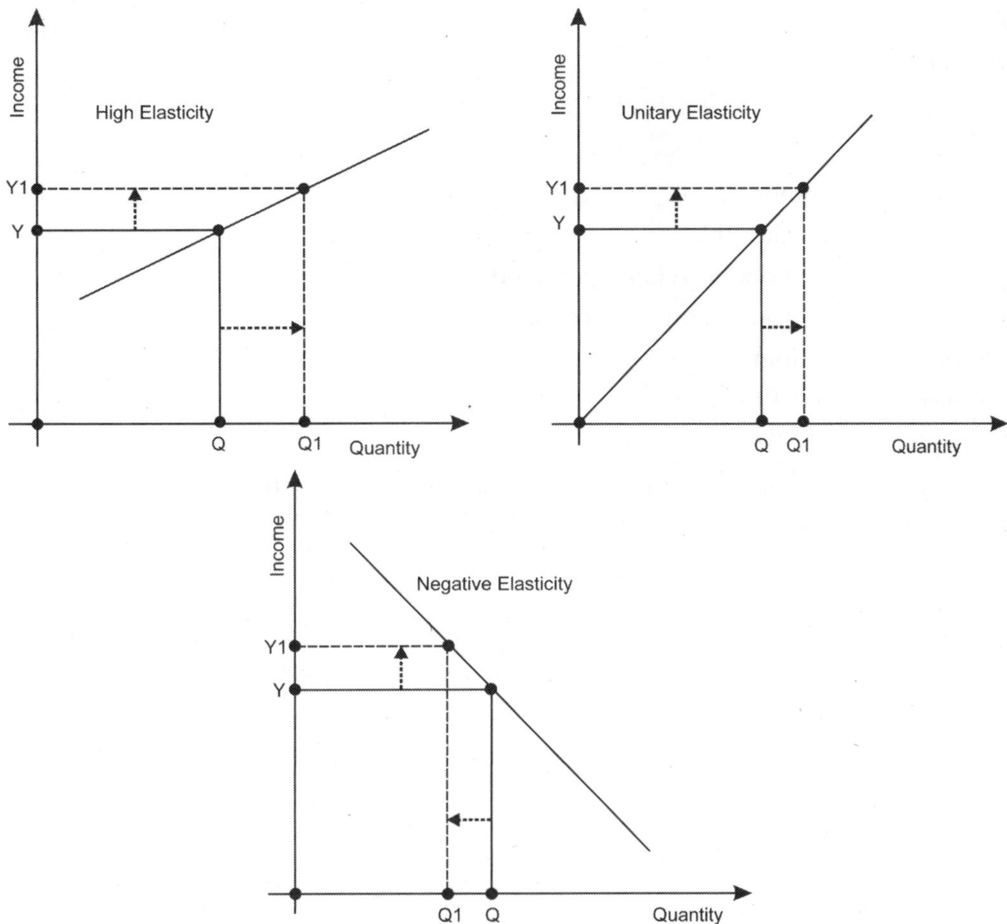

Cross Elasticity of Demand

The degree of responsiveness in the quantity demanded for a commodity 'A', as a result of change in price of commodity 'B'.

$$\text{Cross Elasticity of Demand} = \frac{\text{\% Change in Quantity Demanded of Commodity A}}{\text{\% Change in Price of Commodity B}}$$

$$\text{Cross Elasticity of Demand} = \frac{\dfrac{\text{Change in Quantity of Commodity A}}{\text{Quantity of Commodity A}}}{\dfrac{\text{Change in Price of Commodity B}}{\text{Price of Commodity B}}}$$

Important Points

- *If Cross Elasticity of Demand is Positive, then goods are Substitute.*
- *If Cross Elasticity of Demand is Negative, then goods are Complementary.*

Supply

Supply Function

$$S_n = f(p_n; p_1, p_2, p_3, p_4, p_5, p_6; F_1, F_2 \ldots F_m, T, G)$$

where

S_n = Supply of Commodity '*n*'.

p_n = Price of Commodity '*n*'.

$p_1, p_2, p_3, p_4, p_5, p_6$ = Price of related commodities

$F_1, F_2 \ldots F_m$ = Prices of all factors of production

T = State of Technology

G = Objective of the Producers

Law of Supply

All other factors remaining constant, an increase in supply leads to a decreased price, while a decrease in supply leads to an increased price.

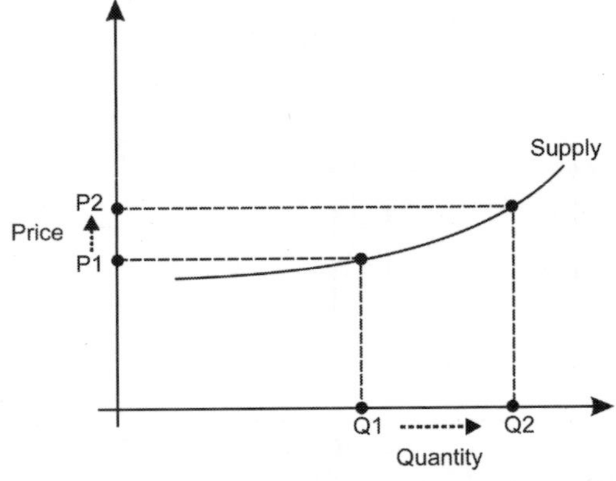

Elasticity of Supply

The degree of responsiveness in the quantity supplied of a commodity, as a result of change in its price. The concept is believed to be developed by Alfred Marshall.

$$\text{Price Elasticity of Supply} = \frac{\text{\% Change in Quantity Demanded of Commodity}}{\text{\% Change in Price of Commodity}}$$

$$\text{Price Elasticity of Supply} = \frac{\dfrac{\text{Change in Quantity of Commodity}}{\text{Quantity of Commodity}}}{\dfrac{\text{Change in Price of Commodity}}{\text{Price of Commodity}}}$$

Factors Determine the Elasticity

1. *Nature of Commodity*: Durability of the commodity (perishable or non-perishable).
2. Cost of Production.
3. Technical conditions obtainable in the industry for production.

4. *Percentage of Income*: The higher the percentage that the product's price is of the consumer's income, the higher the elasticity.

5. *Time Factor*:

- *Perfectly Elastic*: Supply changes even without change in price.
- *Perfectly Inelastic*: Supply never changes with change in price.

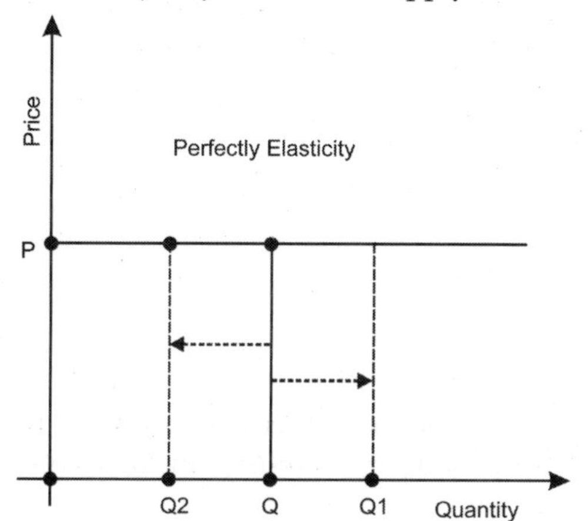

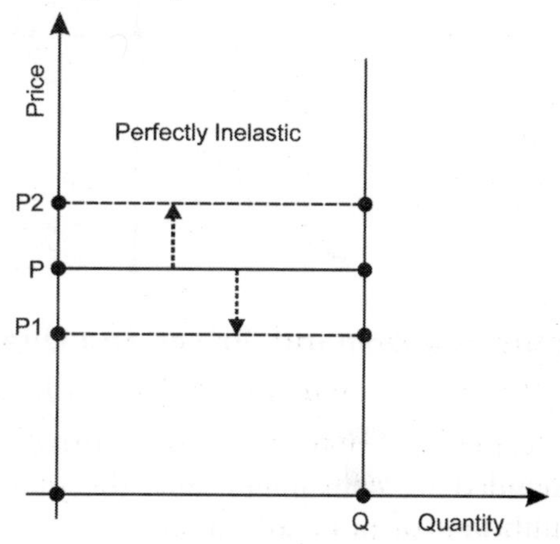

- *Unitary Elastic*: When percentage change in supply is the same as percentage change in price.
- *Elastic*: When percentage change in supply is more than percentage change in price.
- *Inelastic*: When percentage change in supply is less than percentage change in price.

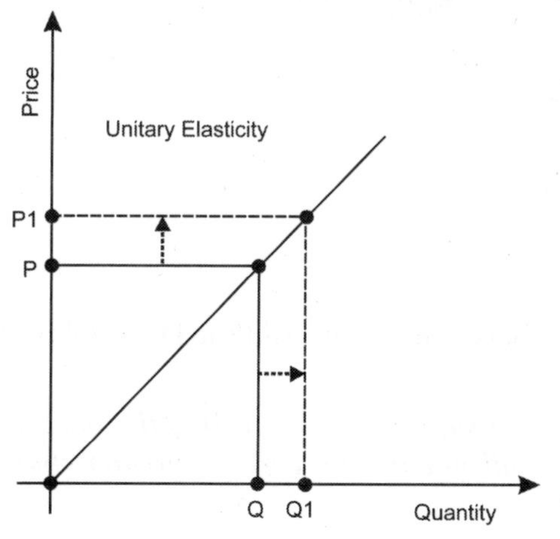

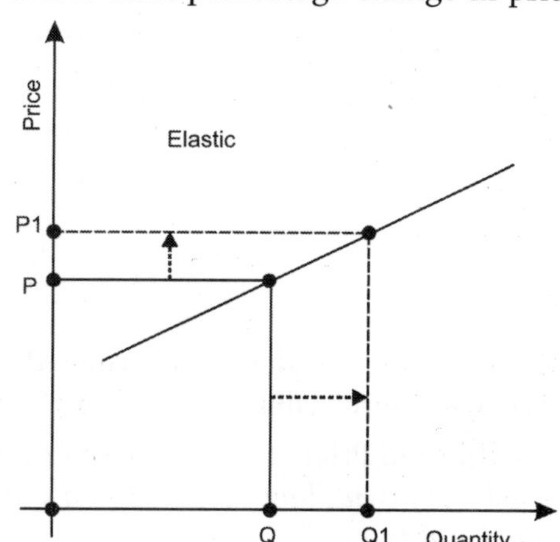

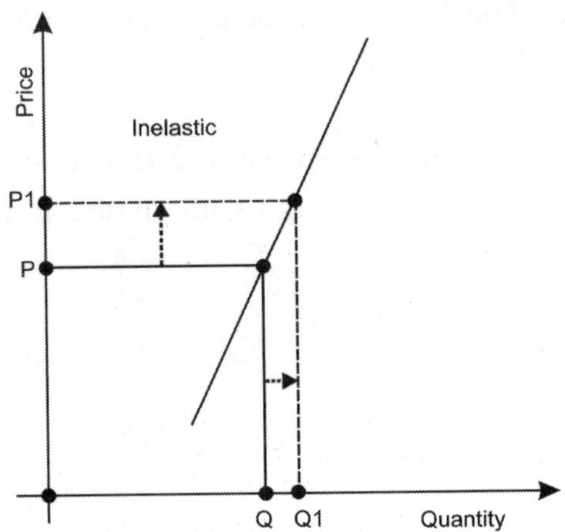

Supply and Demand, Prices and Quantities

It is an economic model based on price and quantity in a market.

It predicts that in a competitive market, price will function to equalize the quantity demanded by consumers, and the quantity supplied by producers, resulting in an economic equilibrium of price and quantity.

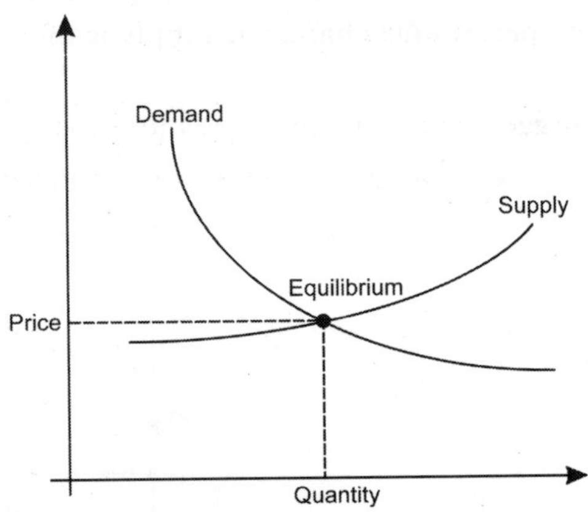

The Price of a product is determined by equilibrium between Supply and the Demand of that product with purchasing power at a given price.

Equilibrium Price: *It is the price at which demand and supply are equal. It is the maximum price a buyer is willing to pay for a commodity and will not in any case be greater than its marginal utility.*

Changes in Market Equilibrium

Demand Curve Shifts

When consumers increase the quantity demanded at a given price, it is referred to as an increase in demand. *The curve will shift outward. Hence, the prices will rise.*

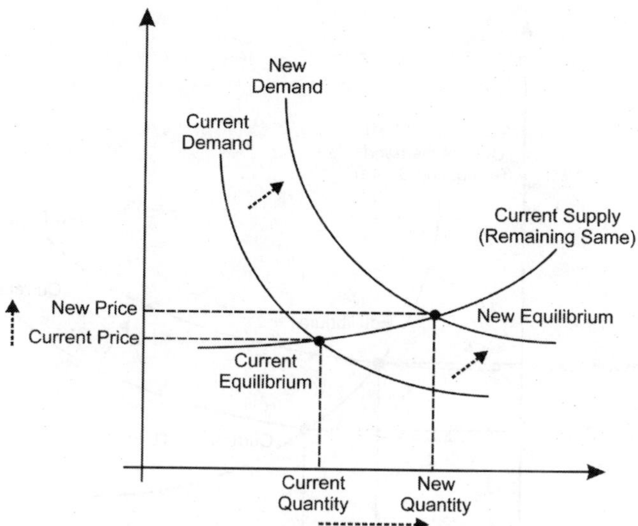

If the demand decreases, then the opposite happens: *An inward shift of the curve. Hence, the prices will fall.*

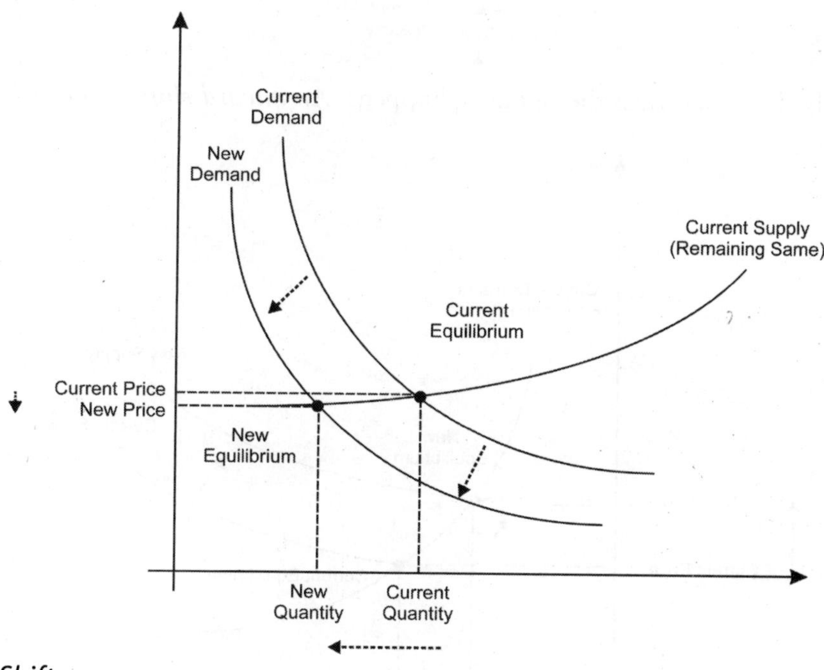

Supply Curve Shifts

When producer increases the quantity supplied at a given price, it is referred to as an increase in supply. *The curve will shift outward. Hence, the prices will fall.*

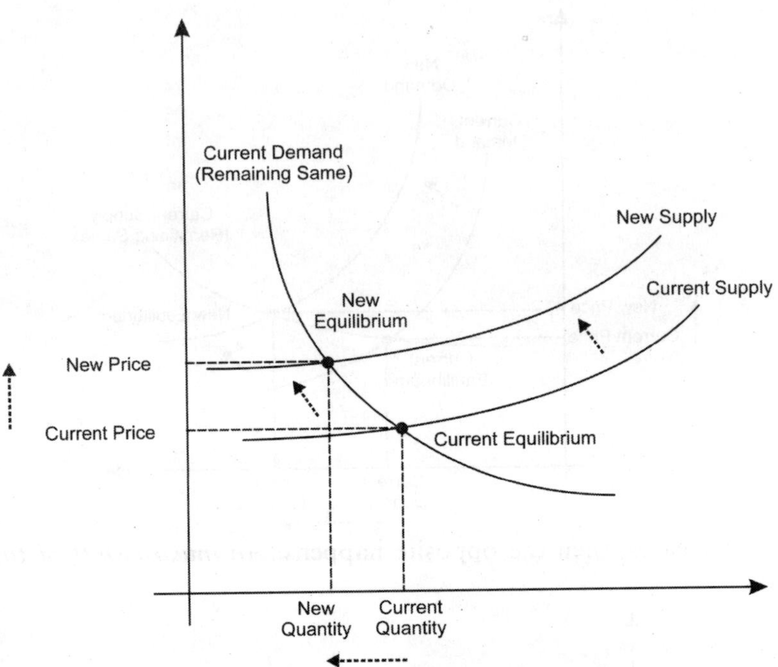

If the supply decreases, then the opposite happens: *An inward shift of the curve. Hence, the prices will rise.*

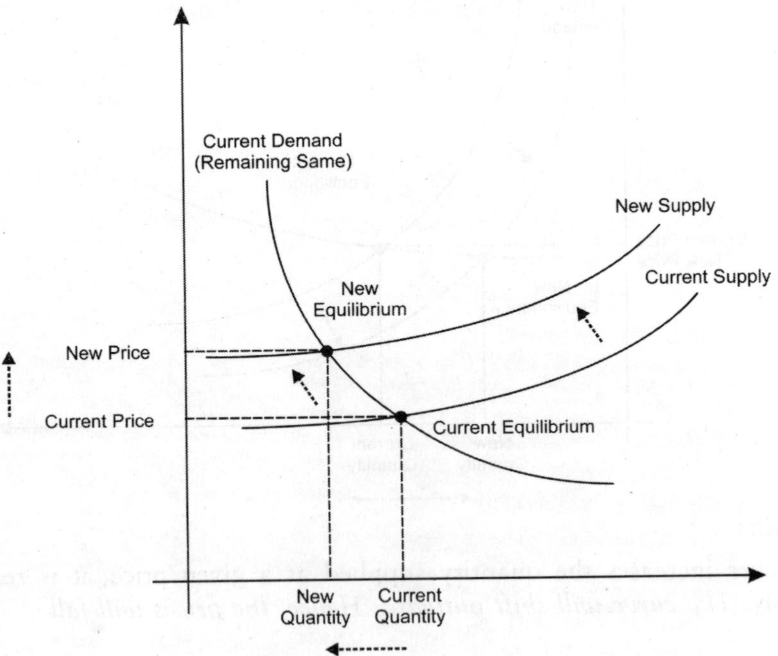

Paradox of Value

Why does Diamond *(not essential for life)* sell at high price and Water *(extremely essential for life)* at low price?

Traditionally, it was unanswerable. However, with the advent of the concept of marginal analysis, an answer was derived.

The demand and supply curve of 'Water' intersect at low price because both marginal cost and marginal utility are very low in case of 'Water', unlike 'Diamond'.

Effect of Tax on Price and Quantity

- Equilibrium price increases while the equilibrium output falls.
- Sales or excise tax are shared among consumers and producers.
- Sharing depends upon elasticity of demand and supply.
- The more inelastic the demand, the burden of tax is borne by the consumer.
- The more elastic the demand, the burden of tax is borne by the producer.
- The more inelastic the supply, the burden of tax is borne by the producer.
- The more elastic the supply, the burden of tax is borne by the consumers.
- With subsidy the equilibrium price falls while the output rises.

Marginal Utility

It is the additional satisfaction or benefit (utility) that a consumer derives from buying an additional unit of a commodity or service.

In simple terms: *Marginal utility is the extra satisfaction generated from consuming one more unit of a good.*

The concept implies that the utility is inversely related to the number of units of that product he already owns.

$$\text{Marginal Utility} = \frac{\text{Change in Total Utility}}{\text{Change in Quantity}}$$

Total Utility is the total satisfaction from the consumption of a product.

Law of Diminishing Returns

The law of diminishing marginal utility states that the value that any household attaches to successive units of a commodity diminishes steadily as its total consumption increases, the consumption of all other commodities being held constant.

The marginal utility to a buyer of a product decreases as he purchases more and more of that product, until the point is reached at which he has no need at all of additional units. The marginal utility is then zero. For example, the first glass of juice will highly satisfy a consumer; however, as he drinks more and more glasses of juice, he will get lesser and lesser satisfaction till the time when he can no longer drink any more juice.

Marginal Utility vs Total Utility Curve

Commodity Units	Total Utility	Marginal Utility
1	50	0
2	80	30 Max
3	100	20
4	120	20
5	125	5
6	130	5
7	139	9
8	144	5
9	146	2
10	147	1
11	147	0
12	147	0

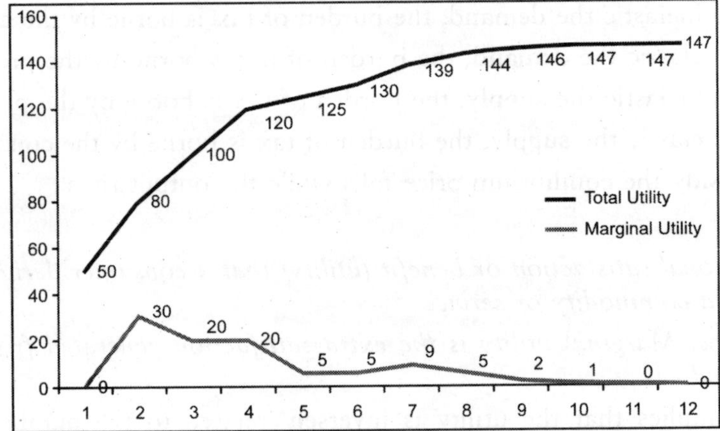

Indifference Curve

It is a curve showing various combinations of two goods that yield equal satisfaction or utility to an individual. The classic indifference curve is drawn downward from left to right and convex to the origin. Because all of the combinations of goods represented by the points on the curve are equally desirable, the consumer would be indifferent towards the combination.

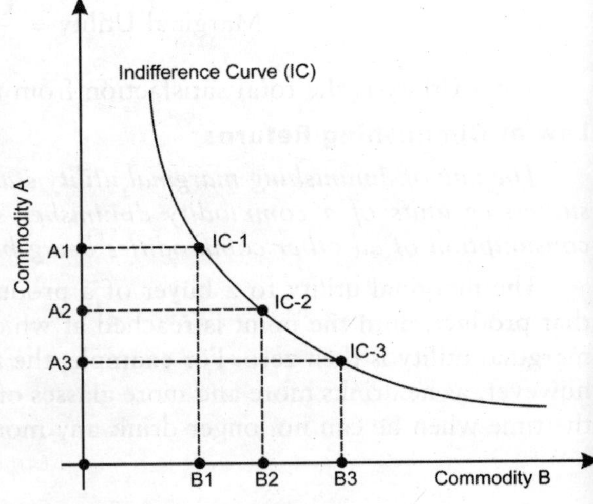

Along the indifference curve (IC), the consumer would be indifferent towards the combination of commodity A and B (A1B1, A2B2 and A3B3). Hence, points IC-1, IC-2 and IC-3 depict equal levels of utility (satisfaction) for various combinations of commodities A and B (A1B1, A2B2 and A3B3).

Properties of Indifference Curve

1. *Downward sloping to the right*: It is because when consumer decides to have more units of one of two goods, he will have to reduce the number of units of other good, if he is to remain on the same indifference curve.
2. *Non-intersecting*: Different IC has different utility.
3. *Convexity*: IC is convex to the origin
4. Higher indifference curve shows higher satisfaction.

Exceptions to the Normal Shape of Indifference Curve

- *Substitute Commodities*: When commodities satisfy the same need.
- *Complementary Commodities*: When commodities have to be consumed together for satisfying a particular need.

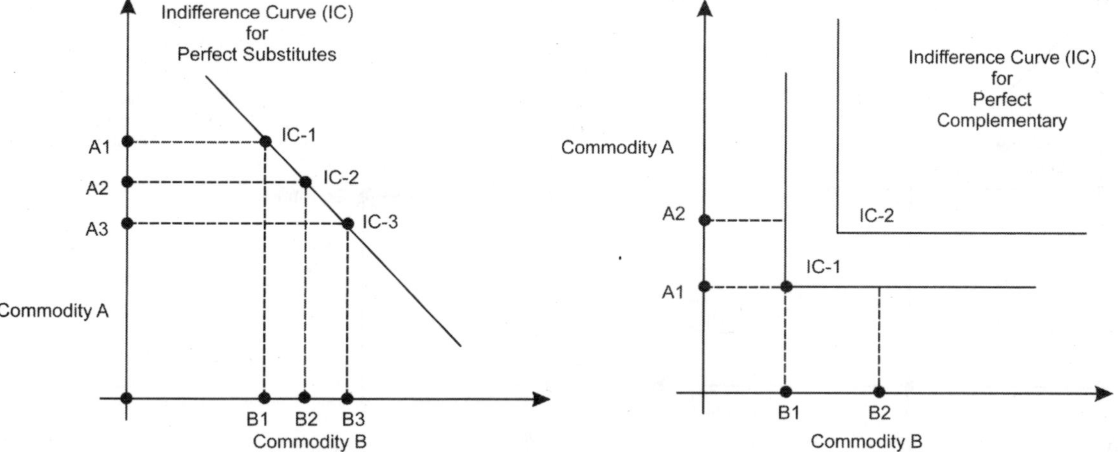

- *Bad Commodities*: The commodities consumer does not like. With rise in income they won't be preferred.
- *Neutral Goods*: When the consumer does not care one way or the other for a particular commodity.

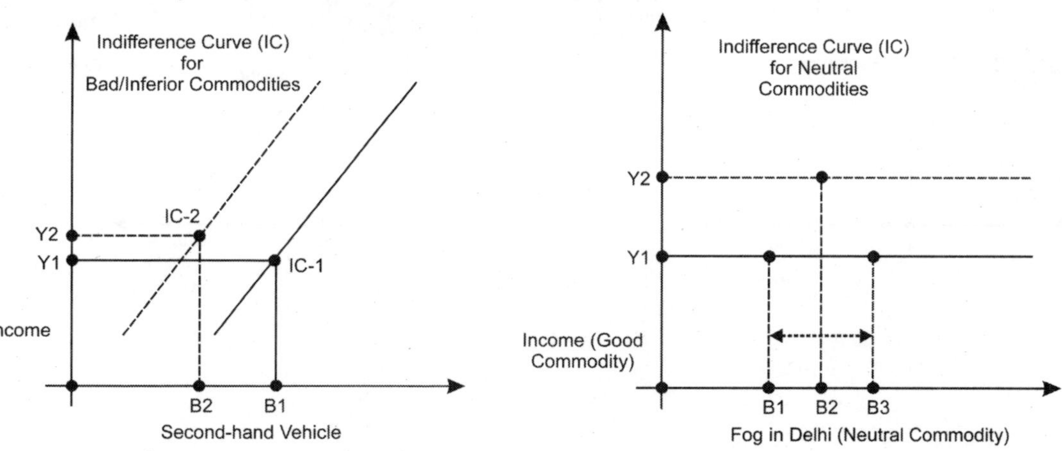

Consumer Surplus

It is a measure of the welfare that people gain from the consumption of goods and services, or a measure of the benefits they derive from the exchange of goods.

—*Tutor 2 u*

In simple terms: *Difference between the price a consumer is prepared to pay and the actual price paid.*

- The majority of demand curves are downward sloping. When demand is inelastic, there is a greater potential consumer surplus because there are some buyers willing to pay a high price to continue consuming the product.

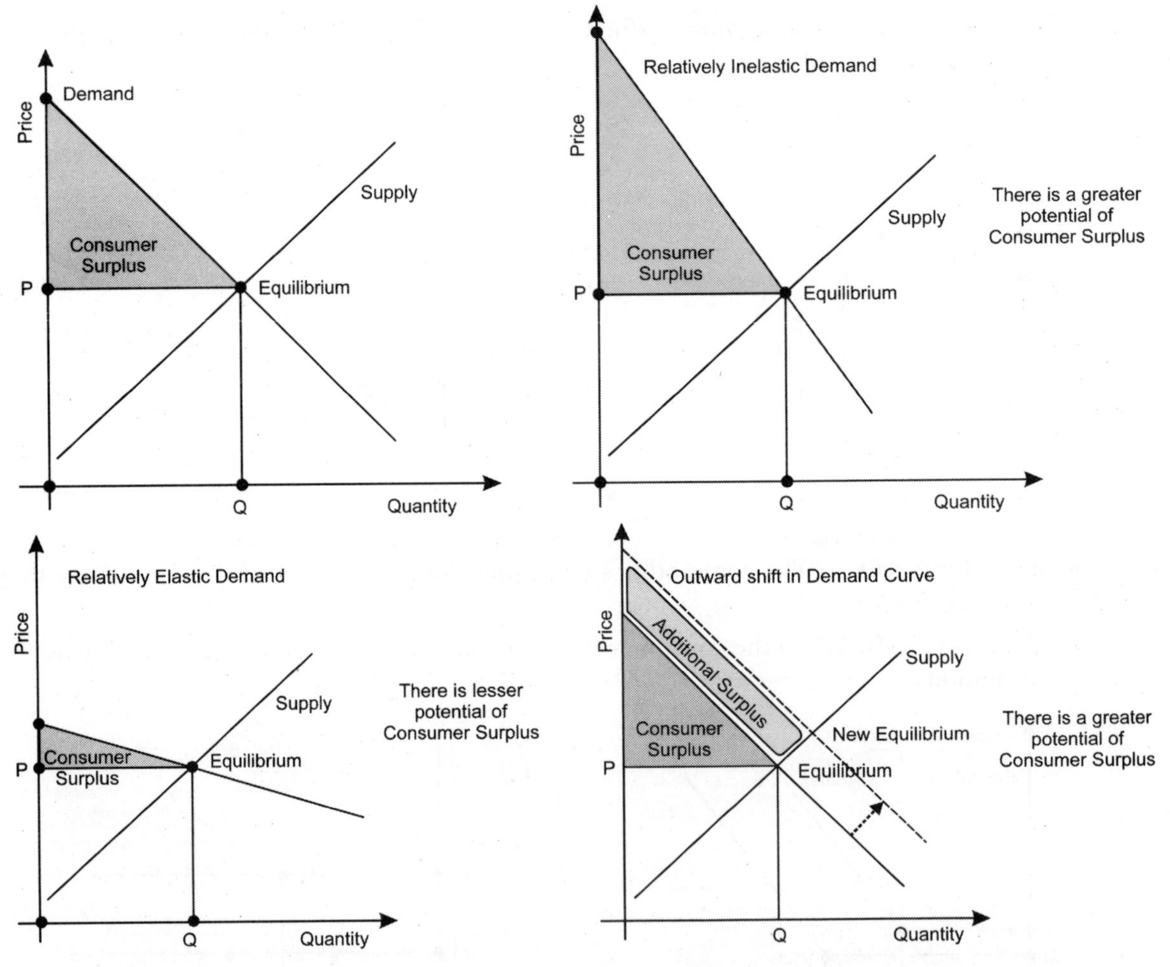

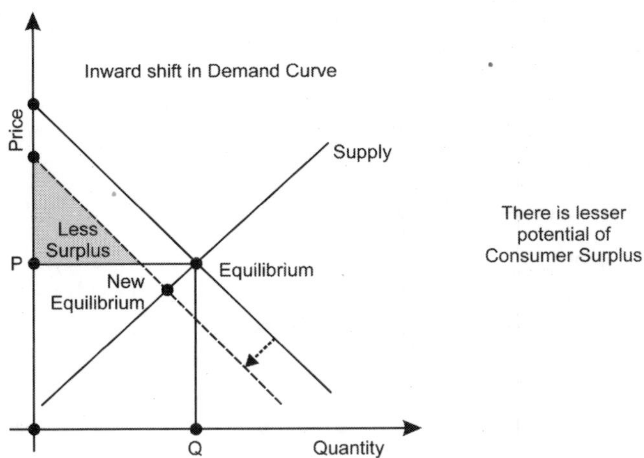

Production Function

It is a function that specifies the output of a firm, an industry, or an entire economy for all combinations of inputs.

—*Tutor Vista*

In simple terms: *The production function relates the output of a firm to the amount of inputs, typically capital and labour.*

$Q = f(X1, X2, X3, ..., Xn)$

where

Q = Output

f = Function

$X1, X2, X3... Xn$ = Factor Inputs (fixed and variable)

- **Short Run Production Function**

The short run production function shows the maximum output the firm can produce when only one of its inputs can be varied, the others remaining fixed.

- **Long Run Production Function**

The long run production function shows the maximum output the firm can produce when all its inputs can be varied.

Isoquants

It is a curve showing the various combinations of two inputs (capital and labour) which can be used to produce a specific level of output.

At different combinations of capital and labour (L1C1, L2C2 and L3C3), we arrive at different levels of output (Is-1, Is-2 and Is-3).

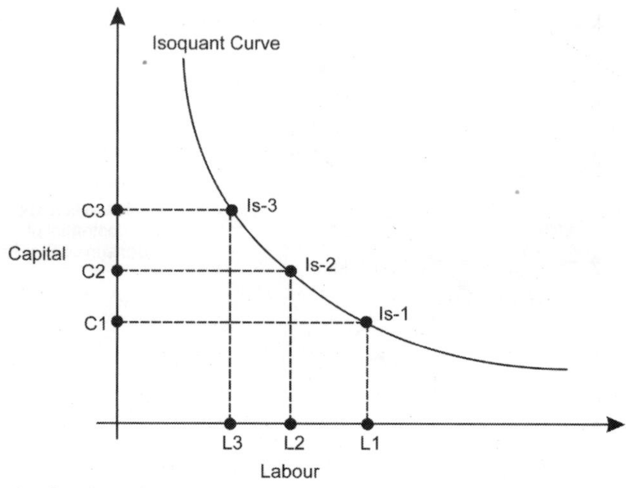

Marginal Rate of Technical Substitution

The slope of an isoquant is called the *marginal rate of technical substitution (MRTS)*. It shows the rate at which one input (e.g. capital) can be substituted for one more unit of the other (labour) even as the level of output remains constant.

Properties of Isoquants

- Isoquants are downward sloping.
- Isoquants are convex to the origin.
- Higher isoquants represent higher levels of output.
- Isoquants are linear (constant slope) when inputs are perfect substitutes.
- If only one combination of inputs exist to produce a given level of output, the isoquant is L-shaped.

Isocost

An isocost line is a line showing combinations of inputs that would yield the same cost. For example All possible combinations of labour and capital that can be purchased for a given total cost.

Returns to Scale

An important property of a long run production function is the concept of returns to scale.

In simple terms: *This refers to what happens to output when the quantity of all inputs is increased by a certain proportion*. There are three possibilities as follow:

- *Increasing Returns*: Output increases by a larger percentage than increase in inputs.
- *Constant Returns*: Output increases by the same percentage as the increase in inputs.
- *Decreasing Returns*: Output increases by a smaller percentage than increase in inputs.

Marginal Physical Product (MPP)

It is the extra amount of output that can be produced when the firm uses one additional unit of an input, holding all other inputs constant.

In simple terms: *It is given by the ratio of the change in total product to the change in the input.*

Increasing, Constant and Diminishing Marginal Returns

- *Increasing Marginal Returns*: When MPP of an input increases as more of the input is used.
- *Constant Marginal Returns*: When MPP of an input remains constant as more of the input is used.
- *Diminishing Marginal Returns*: When MPP of an input decreases as more of the input is used (i.e. "law" of diminishing returns).

Relationship between MRTS and MPP

The marginal rate of technical substitution between two inputs is equal to the ratio of the marginal physical products of the inputs.

Economic Region of Production

- Ridge lines are lines which connect all the points where MP_K (Marginal Production of Capital) and MP_L (Marginal Production of Labour) are zero.
- The region between the ridge lines is called the economic region of production.
- In the long run, a profit-oriented firm will never employ input combinations outside the ridge lines.

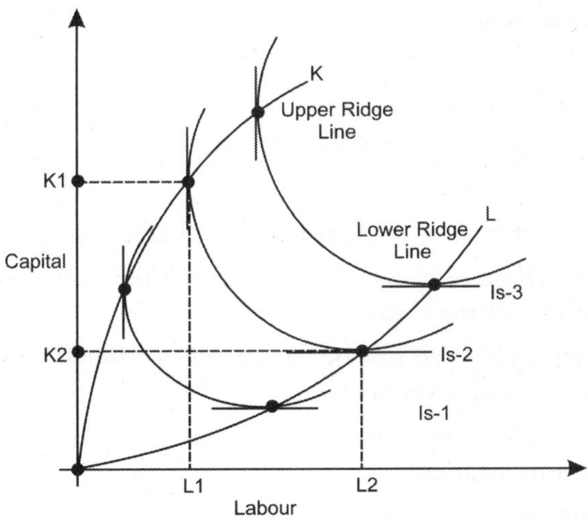

Expansion/Growth Path

- Given the slope of the isocost line (input price ratio); each isoquant has a unique least-cost combination point.
- A least-cost point occurs whenever an isocost line is tangent to an isoquant.
- These points can be connected to form an expansion path.
- In the long run, the firm will expand by moving out the path that connects these points.

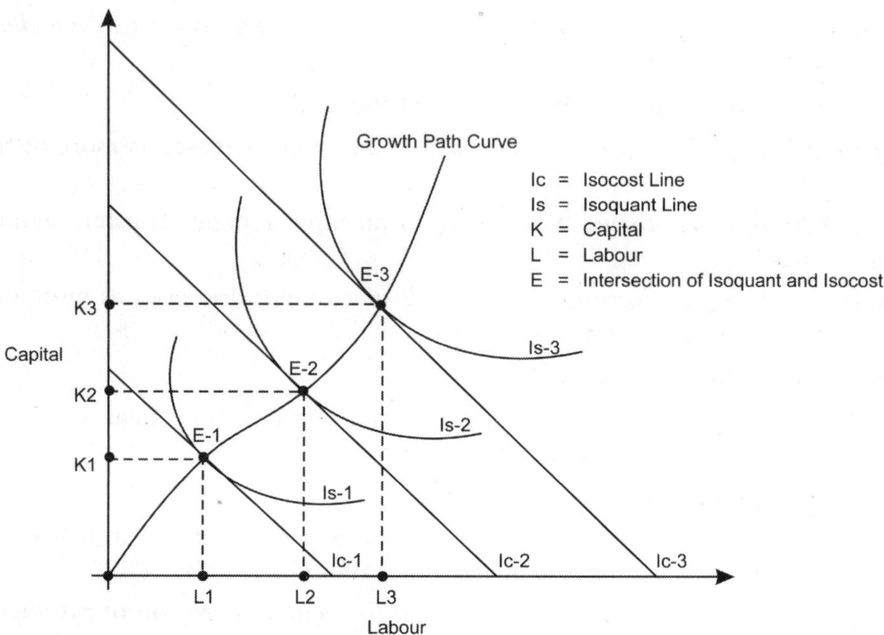

☛ Tip to Learn

- *MP_K = Change in Production/Change in Capital Employed.*
- *MP_L = Change in Production/Change in Labour Employed.*

Theory of Costs

The burden sustained in order to perform a certain activity, to carry out a certain production or to achieve certain goals is called "Cost".

Cost Categories

1. *Actual Costs*: These refer to cost incurred in real transactions.

2. *Opportunity Costs*: These refer to the alternative taken into consideration to choose the line of activity which minimizes the costs.

3. *Discretionary Costs*: They need not be for current production, however, they correspond to strategic goals (e.g. advertising campaign).

4. *Production Costs*: They are usually classified according to their responsiveness to different levels of production attained.

5. *Fixed Costs*: They are generally one time costs and are simply not responsive to production levels.

6. *Variable Costs*: They grow with higher levels of production (proportionally or not).

7. *Total Costs*: They are the sum of all costs (Total Cost = Fixed Cost + Variable Cost × Quantity of Goods Produced).

8. *Average Cost*: Total costs divided by the quantity produces (Total Cost/Quantity of Goods Produced).

9. *Marginal Costs*: They indicate by how much the total costs change because of modification in the production level by one unit.

10. *Sunk Costs*: They are investment costs which are incurred before a certain activity takes place and cannot be recovered by the possible sale of the goods they produced (e.g. research and development)

☛ Tip to Learn

- *For low levels of production, fixed costs are major determinants of average costs.*
- *For high levels of production, variable costs dominate.*

Cost Function

In simple terms: *It is the relationship between product and costs.*

Formula

TC = FC + VC

where

TC = Total Cost

FC = Fixed Cost

VC = Variable Cost

The Costs Model

- Static
- Dynamic (in long or short intervals)

In case of short-term dynamic model, it is assumed that technical conditions, organizational conditions, the structure of products etc. are fixed.

In long-term dynamic models, we try to figure out the influence of changes in technology and work organization on the production level.

Long-Run and Short-Run Cost Functions

- In the long run, the firm can vary all its inputs.
- In the short run, some of the inputs are fixed.

In the diagram, F1 and F2 represent the fixed costs at different levels of output. Similarly, V1 and V2 represent variable cost at different levels of output.

The total cost T1 is arrived by combining F1 and V1. Likewise, T2 from F2 and V2.

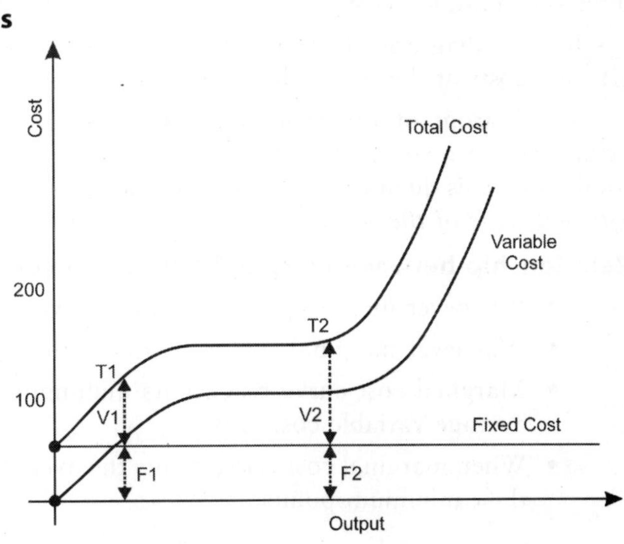

Cost Curves

In simple terms: *It is a graph of the costs of production as a function of total quantity produced.*

- **Average Total Cost Curve**

It is constructed to depict the relation between cost per unit and the level of output (ceteris paribus).

- **Long Run Average Cost Curve**

It depicts per unit cost of producing a good or service in the long run when all inputs are variable.

- **Short Run Average Cost Curve**

When at least one factor of production is fixed, this occurs at the optimum capacity where it has enjoyed all the possible benefits of specialization and no further opportunities for decreasing costs exist.

Cost Curves and Their Shapes

- The average total cost curve is U-shaped.
- At very low levels of output average total cost is high because fixed cost is spread over only a few units.
- Average total cost declines as output increases.
- Average total cost starts rising because average variable cost rises substantially.

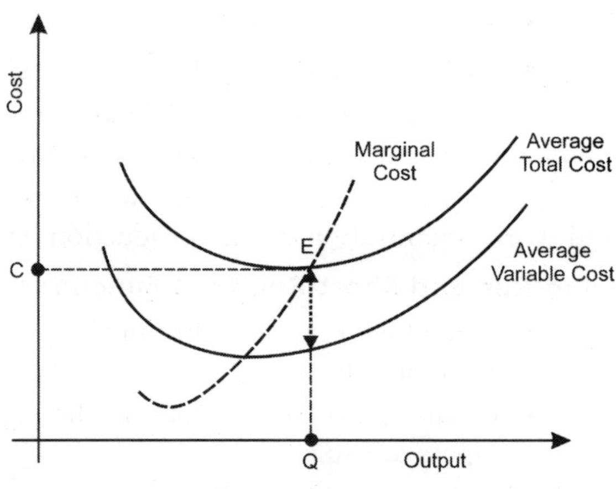

Efficient Productivity

It happens when its factors of production are combined in such a way that the average cost of production is at lowest point and intersects marginal cost.

In the diagram, E represents the most efficient costs at the output level Q.

The bottom of the U-shaped ATC curve occurs at the quantity that minimizes average total cost. This quantity is sometimes called the *efficient scale of the firm.*

Relationship between Marginal Cost and Average Total Cost

- Whenever marginal cost is less than average total cost, average total cost is falling.
- Whenever marginal cost is greater than average total cost, average total cost is rising.
- Marginal cost curve reaches its minimum point before the average total cost and the average variable cost curve.
- When marginal cost rises, it cuts the average variable cost and the average total cost at their minimum points.

Economies and Diseconomies of Scale

- Economies of scale refer to the property whereby long run average total cost falls as the quantity of output increases.
- Diseconomies of scale refer to the property whereby long run average total cost rises as the quantity of output increases.
- Constant returns to scale refer to the property whereby long run average total cost stays the same as the quantity of output increases.

Market Structure (Market Form)

1. *Perfect Competition*: Large number of firms producing a standardized product.
2. *Monopolistic Competition*: Large number of independent firms which have a very small proportion of the market share.
3. *Oligopoly*: A market dominated by small number of firms which own more than 40 per cent of the market share.
4. *Oligopsony*: A market dominated by many sellers and a few buyers.
5. *Monopoly*: Only one player (firm/producer) of a product or service in the market.
6. *Duopoly*: Industry dominated by two large firms.
7. *Natural Monopoly*: A firm is a natural monopoly if it is able to serve the entire market demand at a lower cost than any combination of two or more smaller, more specialized firms.
8. *Monopsony*: When there is only one buyer in a market.

Determinants of Market Structure

- Freedom of entry and exit.
- Nature of the product—identical, differentiated.
- Control over supply/output.
- Control over price.
- Barriers to entry.

Demand Curve Under Different Market Structure

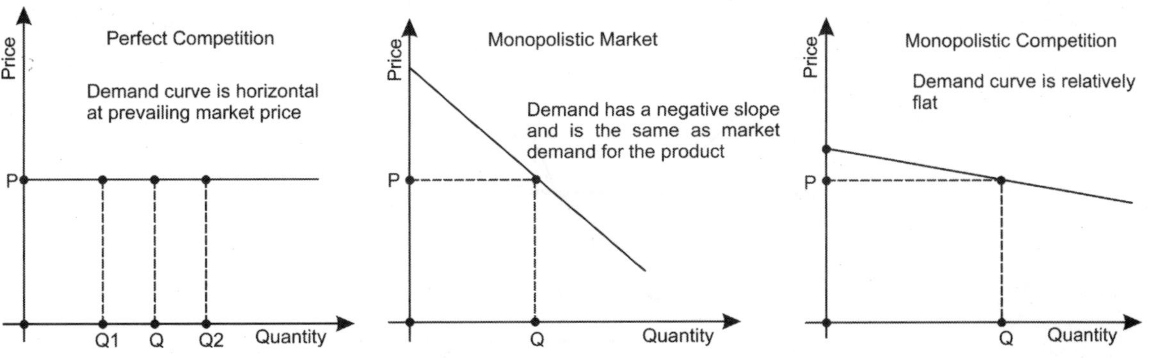

Equilibrium of a Firm in Short Run

- MC = MR
- MC Curve cuts MR Curve from bottom

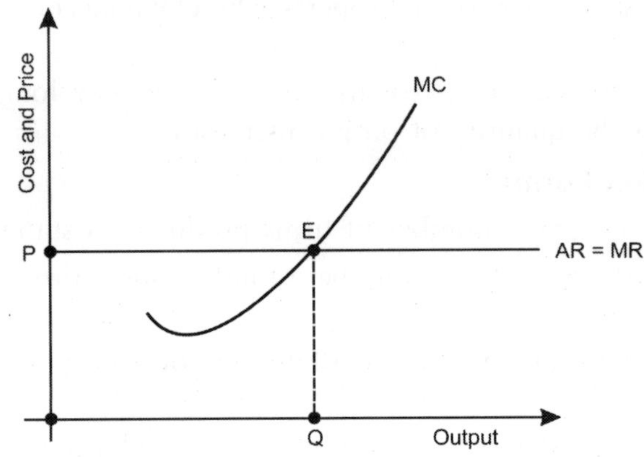

Equilibrium of a Firm in Long Run

- P = MR = LMC = LAC
- SMC = LMC and SAC = LAC

where

MC = Marginal Cost
SMC = Short Run Marginal Cost
LMC = Long Run Marginal Cost
MR = Marginal Revenue
SAC = Short Run Average Cost
LAC = Long Run Average Cost
P = Price

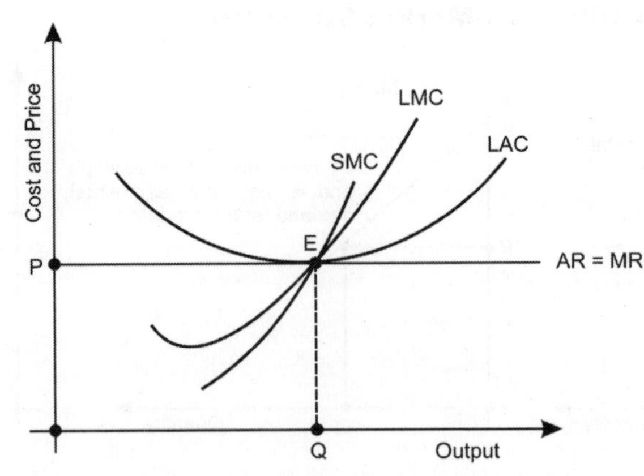

MACROECONIMICS

It is the study of the overall aspects and workings of a national economy such as income, output, and the interrelationship among the diverse economic sectors.

In simple terms: *It is the study of the economy as a whole.*

Main Issues of Macroeconomics

Long Run Economic Growth

- Natural resources
- Labour resources
- Capital resources

Business Cycles or Fluctuations:

- Business cycles are the short run contractions.
- Expansions in economic activity.

Unemployment

Unemployment is the number of people who are available for work and actively seeking work but cannot find jobs.

Inflation/Deflation

- Inflation is a persistent rise in the general price level.
- Hyperinflation is an extremely high rate of inflation.
- Deflation is a persistent decline in the general price level.

The International Economy

- An **open economy** has extensive trading and financial relationships with other national economies.
- A **closed economy** has limited (or no) trading and financial relationships with other national economies.
- Trade imbalances are the differences between exports and imports.
  (i) Trade surplus occurs when exports exceed imports.
  (ii) Trade deficit occurs when imports exceed exports.

Macroeconomic Policy

- **Fiscal policy** is the decisions made about the levels of government spending and tax rates.
- **Monetary policy** is the growth of money supply, determined by a nation's central bank.
- **Positive analysis** examines the economic consequences of a policy.
- **Normative analysis** determines whether a policy should be used.

Conditions for Usefulness of Theory and Models

- The reasonableness of assumptions.
- The possibility of being applied to real problems.

- Whether there are empirically testable implications.
- Whether the theoretical results are consistent with real world data.

Approaches to Macroeconomic Theory

- Classical
  - (i) The economy works well on its own.
  - (ii) The "invisible hand" is the idea that if there are free markets and individuals conduct their economic affairs in their own best interest; the overall economy will work well.
  - (iii) Wages and prices adjust rapidly to get to equilibrium.
  - (iv) One conclusion is that the government should have only a limited role in the economy.
- Keynesians
  - (i) Keynes concluded that persistent unemployment occurred because wages and prices are slow to adjust so that markets can remain out of equilibrium for long periods.
  - (ii) One conclusion is that government should intervene to restore full employment more quickly.
- Unified Approach
  - (i) A single model of the macroeconomy to present both classical and Keynesian ideas.
  - (ii) The model is built on three aggregate markets—the labour market, the goods market, the asset market.
  - (iii) In the long run:
    - (a) Classical believe wages and prices are perfectly flexible.
    - (b) Keynesians believe wages and prices are perfectly flexible.
  - (iv) In the short run:
    - (a) Classical assume flexible wages and prices.
    - (b) Keynesians assume wages and prices are slow to adjust.

Long Run Economic Growth

Long-term economic growth is a result of increasing the quantity and quality of the factors of production in the economy. Growth is determined by the capacity of the economy to increase output and this is determined by the rate of growth of productivity of both capital and labour.

An outward shift in the long run aggregate supply curve for an economy shows an increase in potential output.

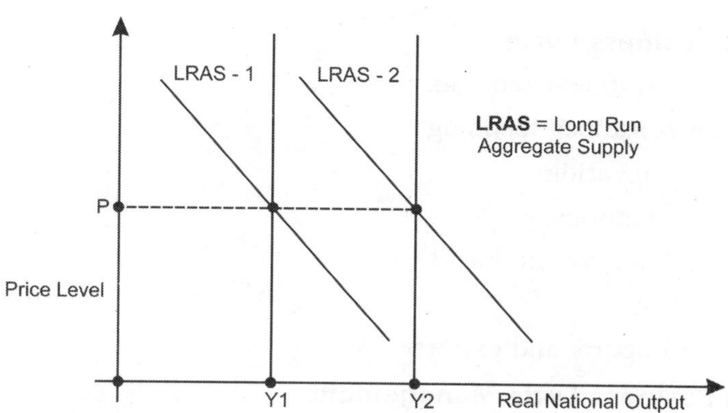

Reasons for Economic Growth

1. *Natural Resources*: Some countries grow because of rich natural resources of land. Saudi Arabia has exploited its oil reserves. The UK, too, is rich in natural resources. Exploitation of natural resources is one pathway to economic growth, although much depends on the market value of these finite resources.

2. *Labour Resources*: Labour is an important source of growth. An increasing population can boost growth, but that may not mean that income per head is growing. The main sources of growth per head of the population are: increasing the quality of the workforce, through better education, training and experience, increases the value of human capital and makes workers more productive.

3. *Capital Resources*: Increasing the stock of capital and making more efficient use of it is another source of growth. Equipping workers with better machines is likely to make those workers more productive, each worker will be able to produce more in the same time.

Business Cycle

In simple terms: *The business cycle is the periodic but irregular up-and-down movements in economic activity, measured by fluctuations in real GDP and other macroeconomic variables.*

Stages in Business Cycle

1. *Recession*: It is a period of reduced economic activity in which levels of buying, selling, production, and employment typically diminish. This is the most unwelcome stage of the business cycle for business owners and consumers alike. A particularly severe recession is known as a depression.

2. *Recovery*: It is the recovery stage of the business cycle is the point at which the economy "troughs" out and starts working its way up to better financial footing.

3. *Growth*: It is a period of sustained expansion. Hallmarks of this part of the business cycle include increased consumer confidence, which translates into higher levels of business activity. Because the economy tends to operate at or near full capacity during periods of prosperity, growth periods are also generally accompanied by inflationary pressures.

4. *Decline*: It is also referred to as a contraction or downturn, a decline basically marks the end of the period of growth in the business cycle. Declines are characterized by decreased levels of consumer purchases (especially of durable goods) and, subsequently, reduced production by businesses.

Factors that Shape Business Cycle

- Irregularity of investment sending.
- Momentum of consumer spending.
- Technological innovation.
- Variations in inventories.
- Fluctuations in government spending.
- Monetary policies.
- Fluctuations in imports and exports.

Keys to Successful Business Cycle Management

- Flexibility of a business plan to change in accordance with the economic environment.
- Adoption of a moderate stance in long-range forecasting.
- Attention to customers and customer satisfaction.
- Need to maintain a high level of objectivity when riding business cycles. Operational decisions based on hopes and desires rather than a sober examination of the facts can devastate a business, especially in economic down periods.
- A thorough study of the business environment to ensure quick response-time.

Unemployment

In simple terms: *A situation where people able, available and are willing to find work, but are not employed.* Unemployment is an important statistic used by the government to gauge the health of the economy.

Causes of Unemployment

- Economy slow down.
- Costs cutting by business concerns for reducing payroll costs.
- Competition in specific industries or companies.
- Poor job performance of employees.

Consequences of Unemployment

- Less consumer spending.
- Recession or even a depression.

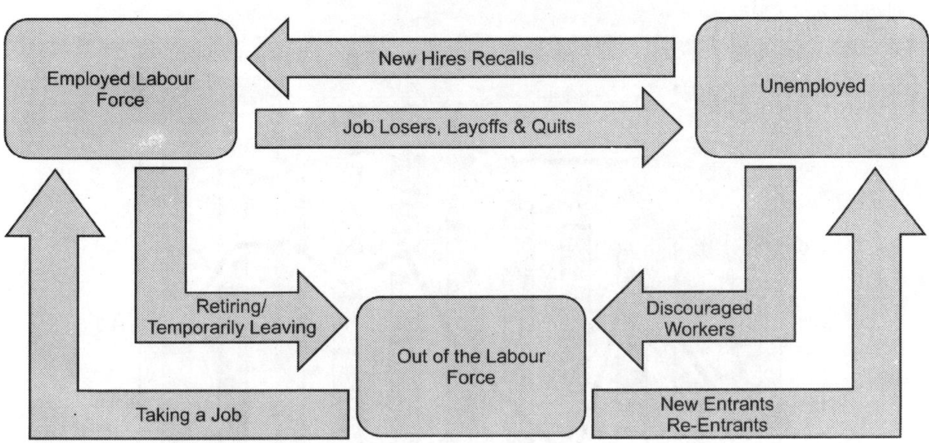

Types of Unemployment

1. *Cyclical Unemployment*: This refers to unemployment that rises during economic downturns and falls when the economy improves. Keynesians argue that this type of unemployment exists due to inadequate effective aggregate demand. It varies with the business cycle.

2. *Frictional Unemployment*: This unemployment involves people in the midst of transiting between jobs, searching for new ones; it is compatible with full employment. It is sometimes called search unemployment and can be voluntary.

3. *Structural Unemployment*: Structural unemployment involves a mismatch between the sufficiently skilled workers looking for jobs and the vacancies available. Even though the number of vacancies may be equal to the number of the unemployed, the unemployed workers lack the skills needed for the jobs, or are in the wrong part of the country or world to take the jobs offered.

4. *Classical Unemployment*: The number of job-seekers exceeds the number of vacancies.

5. *Hidden Unemployment*: Hidden or covered unemployment is the unemployment of potential workers that is not reflected in official unemployment statistics, due to the way the statistics are collected. In many countries, only those who have no work but are actively looking for work (and/or qualifying for social security benefits) are counted as unemployed. Those who have given up looking for work (and sometimes those who are on government "retraining" programmes) are not officially counted among the unemployed, even though they are not employed.

6. *Hardcore Unemployment*: Hardcore unemployment accounts for those unable to work due to mental or physical characteristics, i.e. disabilities.

Global Unemployment Trends, 1998-2008*

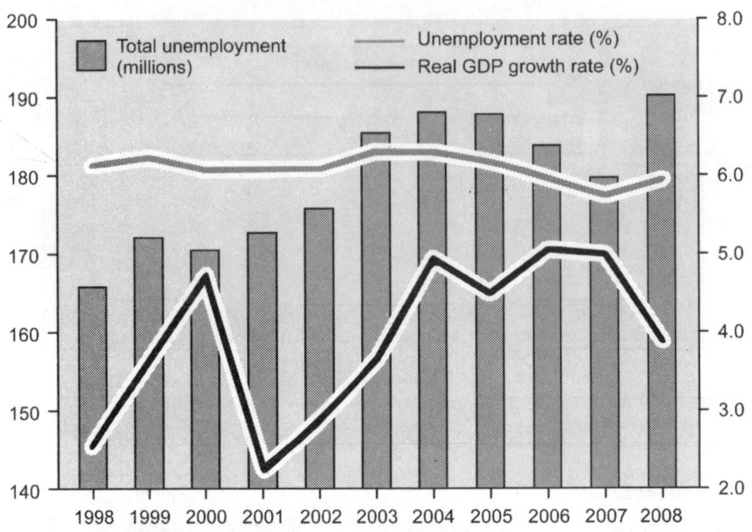

* 2008 are preliminary estimates.

Source: ILO, *Trends Econometric Models*, December 2008

Global Employment Trends, 1998-2008*

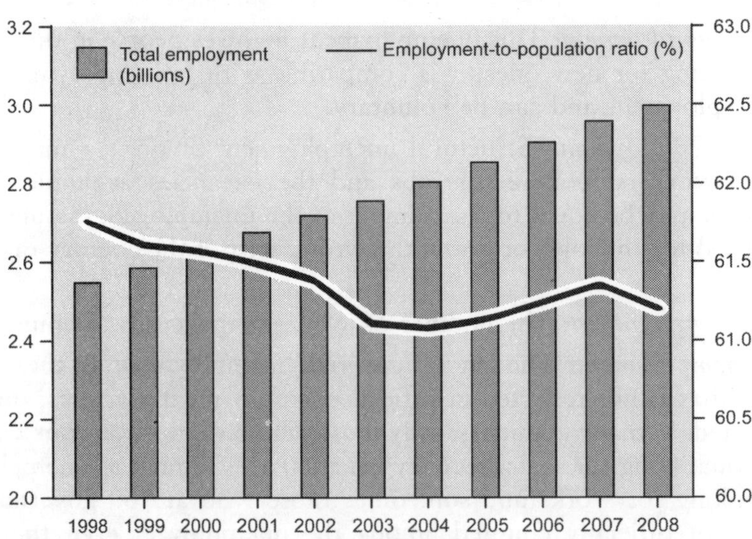

* 2008 are preliminary estimates.

Source: ILO, *Trends Econometric Models*, December 2008

Regional Shares in Employment Creation in 2008*

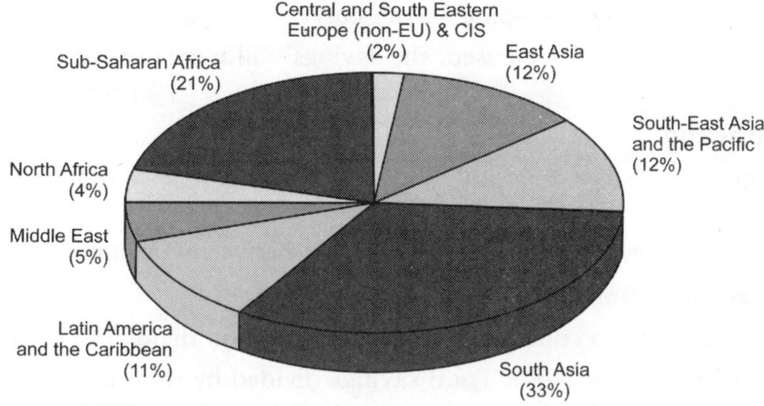

* 2008 are preliminary estimates.

Source: ILO, *Trends Econometric Models*, December 2008

Determinants of Employment

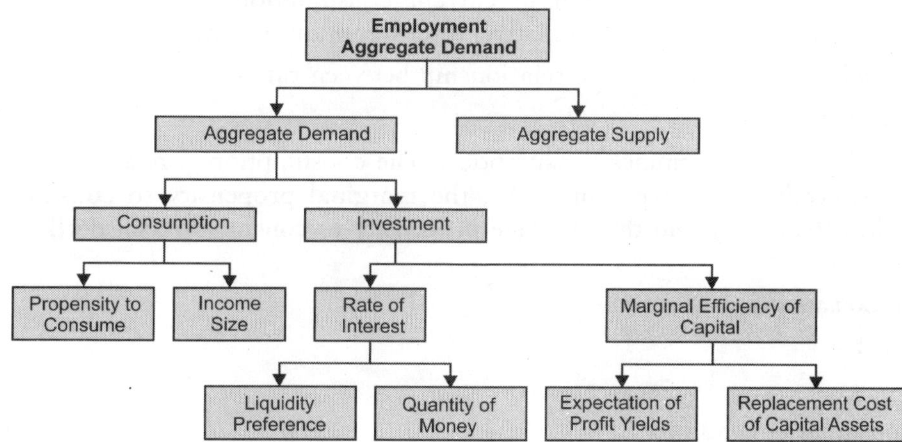

Determinants of Rate of Interest

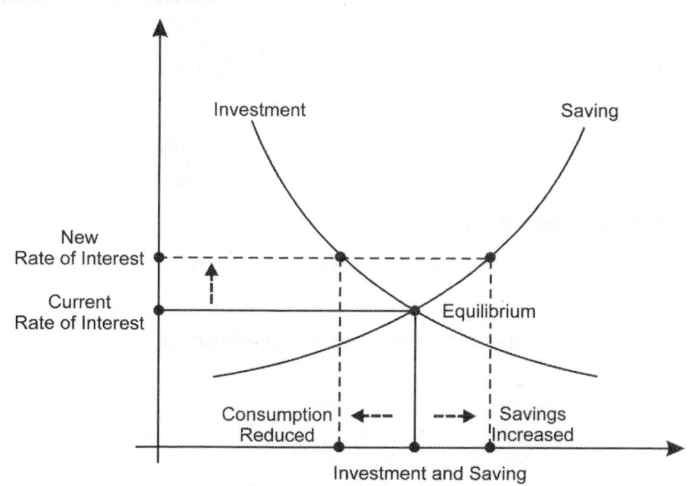

The market rate of interest is determined by the intersection of the downward sloping investment curve and the upward sloping saving curve.

In case the rate of interest is increased, the savings will increase and the consumption will decrease.

Consumption Function

In simple terms: *Developed by John Maynard Keynes, it is a function used to express consumer spending.*

A consumption function highlights the connection between consumption and income.

Key Consumption Definitions

- Average propensity to consume = Total consumption divided by total income
- Average propensity to save = Total savings divided by total income

Classical Views

The level of consumption was determined by the rate of interest. Increase in the rate of interest, increases saving by reduction in current consumption and when rate of interest decreases, the saving also decreases and current consumption increases.

In a nutshell, there was an inverse relationship between rate of interest and consumption.

Keynesian Views

The level of income determines consumption. The consumption is relatively unaffected by interest rate. According to Keynesian views, the marginal propensity to consume (MPC) is positive and less than unity and that average propensity to consume (APC) declines as income increases.

- **Keynesian Consumption Function**

$C = a + c\ Yd$

where

C = Consumer expenditure

a = Autonomous consumption. This is the level of consumption that would take place even if income was zero.

c = It is the marginal propensity to consume (the change in consumption divided by the change in income).

There is a positive relationship between disposable income (Yd) and consumer spending (Ct). As income rises, so does total consumer demand.

Average Propensity to Consume (APC)

In simple terms: *The ratio of consumption expenditure to any particular level of income, i.e. $APC = C/Y$.*

APC declines as income increases due to the proportion of income spent on consumption decreases.

Average Propensity to Save (APS)

In simple terms: *It is the ratio of saving to any particular level of income, i.e. APS = C/Y. APS increases as income increases. APS curve is an upward sloping curve.*

Relationship between APC and APS

- APC + APS = 1
- APC = 1 – APS
- APS = 1 – APC

Marginal Propensity to Consume (MPC)

In simple terms: *It is the ratio of change in consumption to the change in income, i.e. MPC = ΔC/ΔY.*

Marginal Propensity to Save (MPS)

In simple terms: *It is the ratio of change in saving to the change in income, i.e. MPS = ΔS/ΔY.*

Relationship between MPC and MPS

- Value of MPC/MPS lay between zero and one, i.e. 0 < MPC < 1 and 0 < MPS < 1
- MPC + MPS = 1
- MPC = 1 – MPS
- MPS = 1 – MPC
- The MPC declines as income increases and MPS increases as income increases.

Relationship between MPC and APC

- As income increases, the MPC as well as the APC both decline, but decline in the MPC is more than the decline in the APC.
- When the MPC is constant, the consumption function is linear, i.e. a straight-line curve. The APC will also be constant only if the consumption function passes through the origin. However, if it does not pass through the origin, the APC will not be constant.
- Over the long run, the MPC is equal to the APC and approximate 0.9.
- The MPC is higher in poor communities and lower in case of rich communities.

Simple Illustration

Income (Y) (in ₹)	Consumption (C) (in ₹)	Saving (S) (in ₹)	Year	MPS (ΔC/ΔY)	MPS (ΔC/ΔY)	MPS + MPS	APC (C/Y)	APC (S/Y)	APC + APS
1,000	600	400	1990	0.50	0.50	1.00	0.60	0.40	1.00
1,200	700	500	1991	0.50	0.50	1.00	0.58	0.42	1.00
1,400	800	600	1992	0.50	0.50	1.00	0.57	0.43	1.00
1,600	900	700	1993	0.50	0.50	1.00	0.56	0.44	1.00
1,800	1,000	800	1994	0.50	0.50	1.00	0.56	0.44	1.00
2,000	1,050	950	1995	0.25	0.75	1.00	0.53	0.48	1.00
2,200	1,070	1,130	1996	0.10	0.90	1.00	0.49	0.51	1.00
2,400	1,070	1,330	1997	0.00	1.00	1.00	0.45	0.55	1.00

Note:
D = Change
MPC = Marginal Propensity to Consume
MPS = Marginal Propensity to Save
APC = Average Propensity to Consume
APS = Average Propensity to Save

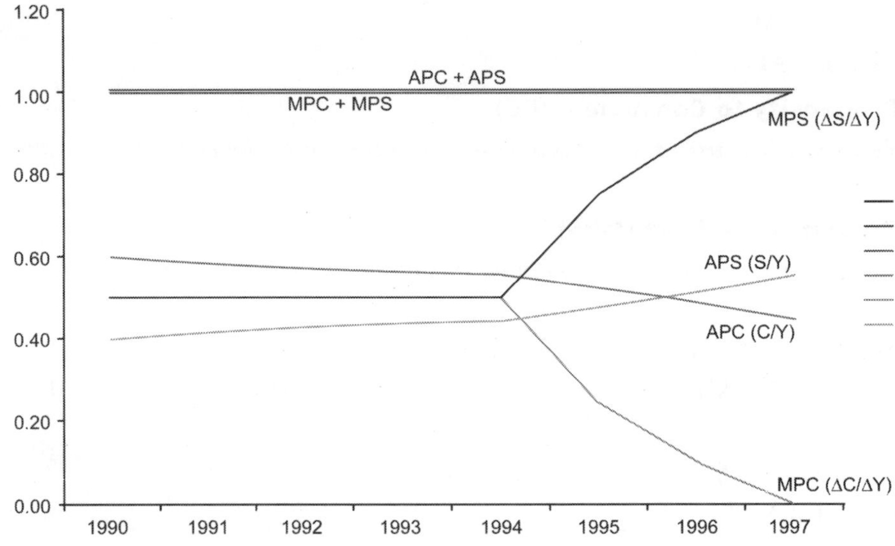

Investment Function

In simple terms: *It explains how the changes in national income induce changes in investment patterns in the national economy.*

Marginal Efficiency of Capital

It refers to how much investment in capital is required to increases output. For example, if the marginal efficiency of capital was 15 per cent and interest rates were 10 per cent, then it is worth borrowing at 10 per cent to get an expected increase in output of 15 per cent. However, if the marginal efficiency of capital is less than interest rates it is not worth investing.

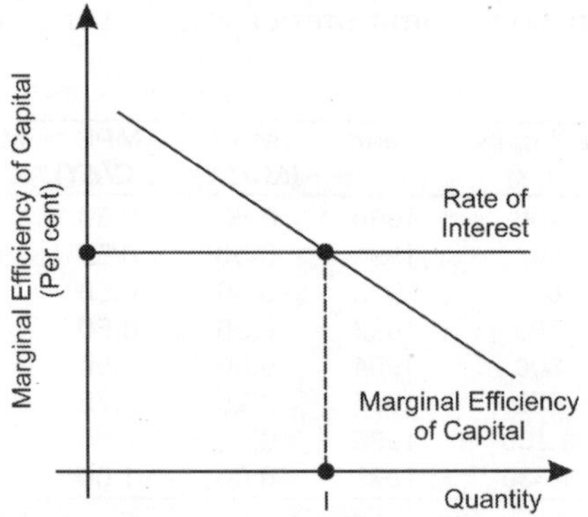

Equilibrium of real planned investment per period is determined by the point of intersection of marginal efficiency schedule and the rate of interest.

Marginal Efficiency of Investment

In simple terms: *It is the expected rates of return on investment as additional units of investment are made under specified conditions and over a stated period of time.*

Inflation

In simple terms: *A persistent increase in the level of consumer prices or a persistent decline in the purchasing power of money, caused by an increase in available currency and credit beyond the proportion of available goods and services.*

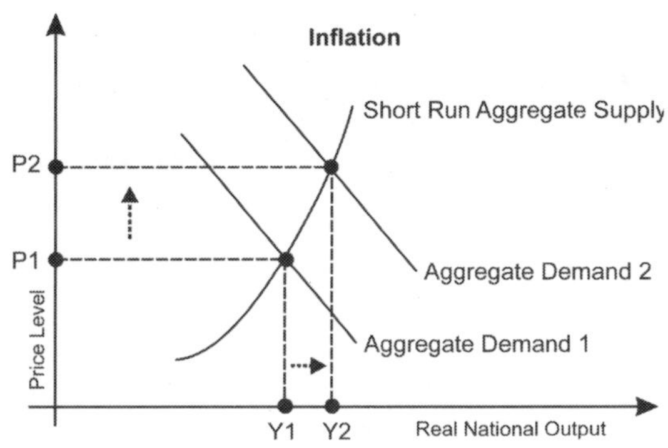

Causes of Inflation

1. *Demand-Pull Inflation*: When the actual demand of goods and services are more than their availability. This shortage of supply enables sellers to raise prices until equilibrium is put in place between supply and demand.

2. *The Cost-Push Inflation*: It is also known as "supply shock inflation". It suggests that shortages to the available supply of a certain good or product will cause a ripple effect through the economy by raising prices through the supply chain from the producer to the consumer.

3. *Role of Money Supply*: It plays a large role in inflationary pressure as well. Monetarist economists believe that if the Federal Reserve does not control the money supply adequately, it may actually grow at a rate faster than that of the potential output in the economy, or real GDP. The belief is that this will drive up prices and hence, inflation. Low interest rates correspond with high levels of money supply and allow for more investment in big business and new ideas which eventually leads to unsustainable levels of inflation as cheap money is available.

4. *Artificial Creation of Inflation*: Inflation can artificially be created through a circular increase in wage earners demands and then the subsequent increase in producer costs which will drive up the prices of their goods and services.

Effects of Inflation

1. A decline in the purchasing power of holdings by individuals and firms.
2. Cost increases in case of payments to workers and pensioners, especially for those with fixed payments.
3. Addition of inefficiencies in the market, hence making it difficult for companies to budget or plan long-term.

4. Adverse effect on productivity as companies is forced to shift resources away from products and services in order to focus on profit and loss from currency inflation.
5. Uncertainties about the future purchasing power of money discourage investment and saving.
6. Rising inflation in one economy will cause its exports to become more expensive and affect the balance of trade.

Deflation

In simple terms: *A persistent decrease in the level of consumer prices or a persistent increase in the purchasing power of money because of a reduction in available currency and credit.*

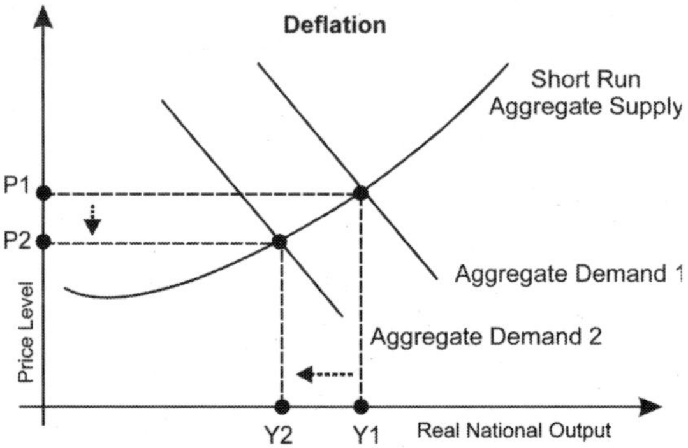

Causes of Deflation

1. *Decrease in the money supply*: In case of an economy based on credit, decrease in money supply will result in a remarkably less lending trend, followed by a sharp decline in the money supply.

2. *Increase in the supply of goods*: Growth in the number of competitors enhances the supply of goods, indicating that the prices must decrease to stabilize demand, thereby bringing in deflation.

3. *Fall in the demand for goods*: A decline in the demand of goods is followed by a decline in the prices, owing to the development of a condition called surplus supply.

4. *Escalation in the demand for money*: According to monetarist viewpoint, 'deflation' occurs when there is a decrease in the velocity of money and/or in the amount of monetary supply per person.

Effects of Deflation

1. Deflation results in the improvement of production efficiency, due to lowering of the overall price of commodities.
2. Deflation discourages both investment and expenditure.
3. According to the monetarist view, 'deflation' affects an economy by decreasing the velocity of money or the number of commercial transactions more or less permanently, hence resulting in contraction of money supply.

Stagflation

In simple terms: *Sluggish economic growth coupled with a high rate of inflation and unemployment.*

Theories of Stagflation

- *Differential Accumulation*: This concept stresses the power by dominant capital groups to beat the average normal rate of return on investment.
- *Neo-Classical Theory*: It asserts that stagflation occurs due to the excessive regulation of the government.
- *Shock Theory*: According to this theory, stagflation occurs due to outside forces of an economy like abrupt increase of oil price influences country's total supply curve.
- *Quality Theories of Stagflation*: According to this theory, central banks play a significant role in maintaining stable prices through management of inflationary anticipation.
- *Quantity Theory*: It states that stagflation occurs because of money supply and not because of demand. The other reason of the occurrence of inflation is the increase of money supply in a period of growing prices.
- *Classical Keynesian Theory and the Phillips Curve*: As per this theory, unemployment brings down demand for goods and services, which ultimately reduce the prices. This establishes the idea that unemployment restricts stagflation.
- *Neo-Keynesian Theory*: It is a modified modern version of Classical Keynesian theory, which is based on two types of inflation (i.e. demand pull and cost push).

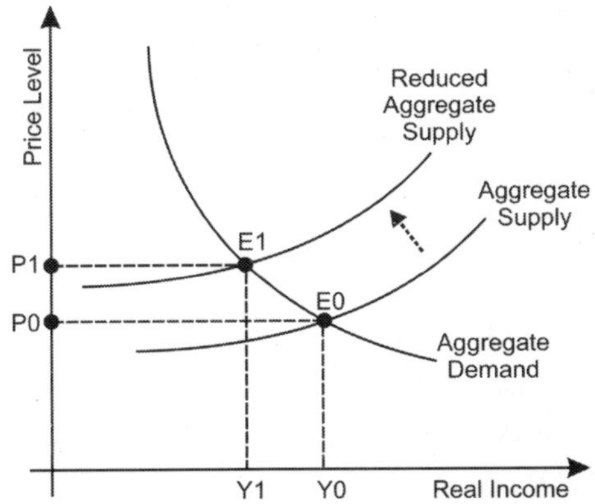

A decrease in the aggregate supply will raise the price level from P0 to P1 and will bring down the output level from Y0 to Y1. This decrease will leads to unemployment.

Demand for Money

Many factors influence our total demand for money balances. The four main factors are:

- The level of prices.
- The level of interest rates.
- The level of real national output (real GDP).
- The pace of financial innovation.

Keynesian Demand for Money—Liquidity Preference

- *The Transaction Demand*: Money used for the purchase of goods and services. The transactions demand for money is positively related to real incomes and inflation.
- *The Precautionary Balance*: To cover unexpected items of expenditure. As with the transactions demand for money, it is positively correlated with real incomes and inflation.
- *Speculative Balances*: Money not held for transaction purposes but in place of other financial assets, usually because they are expected to fall in price.

The Total Demand for Money = Transactions + Precautionary + Speculative Demands.

(There is an inverse relationship between the rate of interest and the speculative demand for money.)

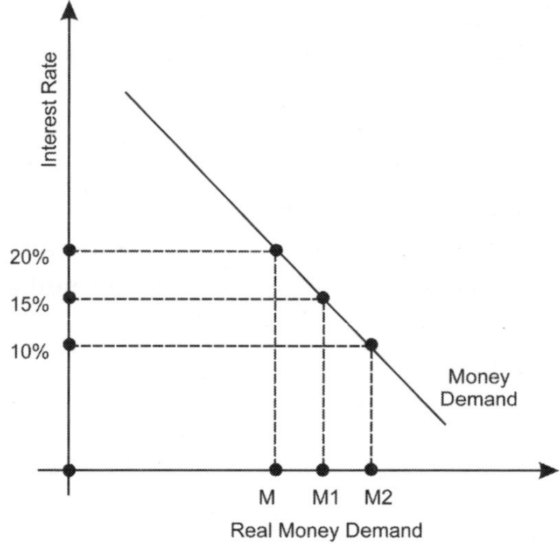

Money Supply

In simple terms: *The total supply of money in circulation in a given country's economy at a given time. There are several measures for the money supply such as M1, M2, M3 and M4.*

- M1 = Currency held by Public + Net Demand Deposits of Banks + Other Deposits of the RBI (C + DD + OD)
- M2 = M1 + Post Office Savings Deposits
- M3 = M1 + Net Time Deposits of Banks
- M4 = M3 + Total Deposits with the Post Office Savings Organization (excluding National Savings Certifications)

National Income

"The national dividend or income consists solely of services as received by ultimate consumers, whether from their material or from their human environment."

—*Irving Fisher*

"National income estimate measures the volume of commodities and services turned out during a given period counted without duplication."

—*National Income Committee of India*

Basic Concepts

- **Gross National Product (GNP):** It is the total value of output (goods and services) produced and income received in a year by domestic residents of a country. It includes profits earned from foreign investments as well.

  GDP = GNP – Net Income Earned from Abroad

- **Gross Domestic Product (GDP):** It is the total value of output (goods and services) produced by the factors of production located within the country's boundary in a year. The factors of production may be owned by either citizens or foreigners.

  GDP = Per Capita Income/Total Population

  Per Capita GDP = Gross Domestic Product/Total Population

- **Per Capita Income:** It is an indicator to show the standard of living of the people in a country.

  Per Capita Income = National Income/Population

- **Net National Product (NNP):** It is arrived at by making some adjustment, with regard to depreciation, in GNP. Decline in the capital assets due to wear and tear is measured as 'capital depreciation'.

  NNP = GNP – Depreciation

- **Net Domestic Product (NDP):** It is arrived from GDP by making adjustment with regard to depreciation in GDP.

  NDP = GDP – Depreciation

- **Factor Cost:** Payments made to various factors of production for their services.
- **Net Indirect Taxes:** Taxes levied on commodities, e.g. sales tax, excise duty, etc.
- **Transfer Payments:** Payments for which no productive services are rendered, e.g. pension, scholarship, unemployment allowance, etc.
- **Subsidy:** It is of transfer payment and is not included in National Income.
- **Intermediate Goods:** Goods which are used for production of other commodities. They are not available for immediate consumption.
- **Final Goods:** The goods which are sold in the market for either final consumption or to be used as intermediate goods for further production.
- **Economic Goods:** Goods which have economic value. They are never free of cost and have limited supply.
- **Non-Economic Goods:** Goods which a gift of nature and are available in abundance. They are free goods.
- **Market Price:** Price at which goods are sold in the market.

  Market Price = Factor Cost + Net Indirect Taxes

- **Net Income from Abroad:** Income attributable to factor services rendered by normal residents to the rest of the world less factor services rendered to them by the rest of the world.
- **Operating Surplus:** In national accounts it is sometimes referred to as "mixed income".

  Operating Surplus = Gross Output – (Intermediate Consumption + Compensation to Employees + Depreciation + Net Indirect Taxes)

Operating Surplus = Gross Value Added at Market Price – (Gross Output – Intermediate Consumption) – Compensation to Employees – Depreciation – Net Indirect Taxes)

Operating Surplus = Net Value Added – Compensation to Employees – Net Indirect Taxes

- **Private Income:** Any type of income received by a private individual or household, often derived from occupational activities.

  Private Income = Income from Domestic Product Accruing to Private Sector + National Debt Interest + Net Income from Abroad + Transfer Payment + Net Transfer from the Rest of the World.

- **Personal Income:** Total income received by a household from all sources.

  Personal Income = Private Income – Corporation Tax – Undistributed Profits

- **Personal Disposable Income:** That part of personal income which is at disposal of individuals for consumption.

  Personal Disposable Income = Personal Income – Direct Taxes – Miscellaneous Receipts from Government

- **Personal Expenditure:** Personal Income – Personal Saving
- **Personal Saving:** Personal Income – Personal Expenditure
- **Closed Economy:** An economy which has no economic relations with other countries of the world. Precisely, no imports and exports.
- **Open Economy:** An economy which has economic relations with other countries of the world.

National Product Calculation and Interrelation (Three Ways to Calculate)

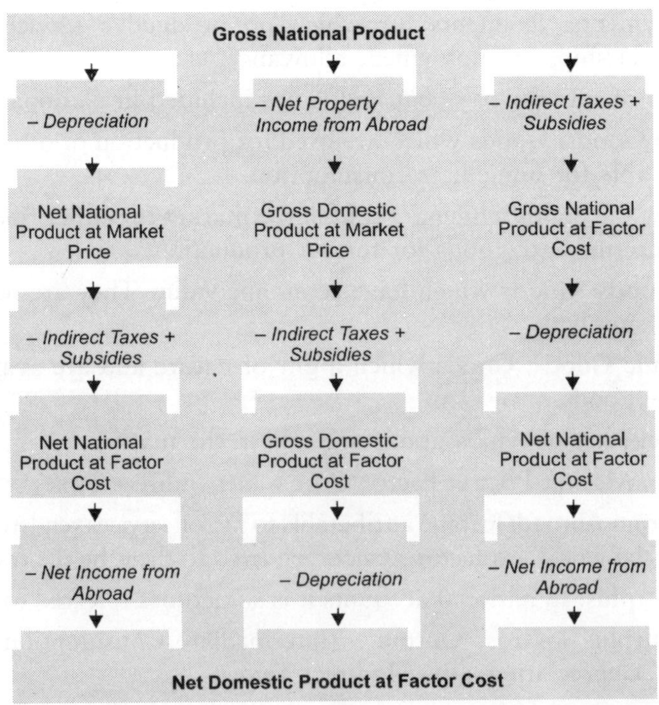

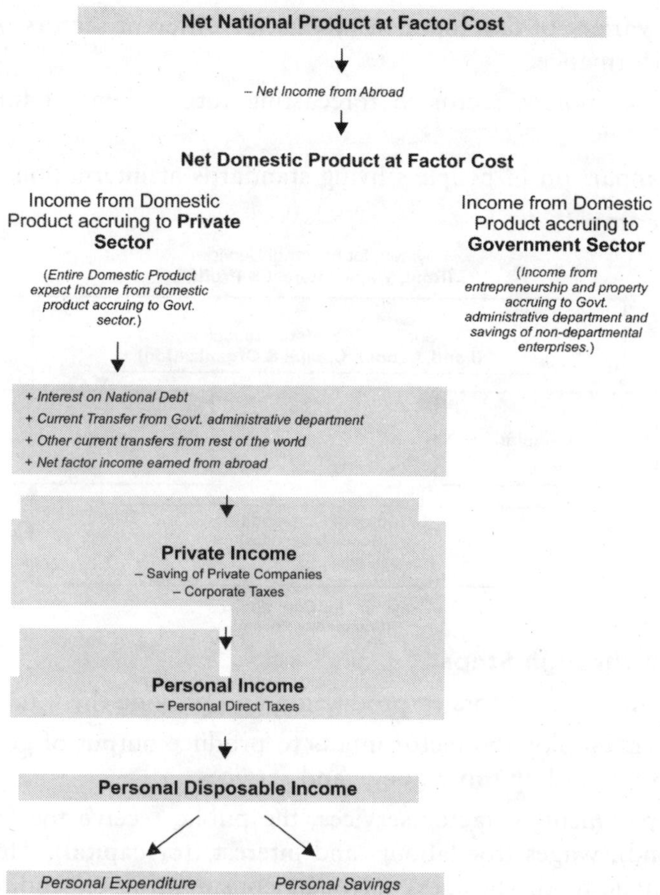

National Income at 'Current Prices' and 'Constant Prices'

- National income arrived from 'current price' includes inflation and taxes.
- National income arrived from 'constant prices' is based on unchanged price (base price) of output. Necessary adjustments are made to eliminate the effect of inflation. It is also called 'real national income'.

Need for the Study of National Income

1. For measuring the size of the economy and level of country's economic performance.
2. For tracing the trend and speed of the economic growth in relation to previous year(s) as well as to other countries.
3. For knowing the structure and composition of the national income in terms of various sectors along with periodical variations in them.
4. For making projection about the future development trend of the economy.
5. For assisting government in formulation development plans and policies to increase growth rates.

6. To set up a variety of development targets for different sectors of the economy based on prior performance.
7. To help the corporate sector in forecasting future demand for their products and services.
8. To make comparison of people's living standards at international levels.

Circular Flow of Income

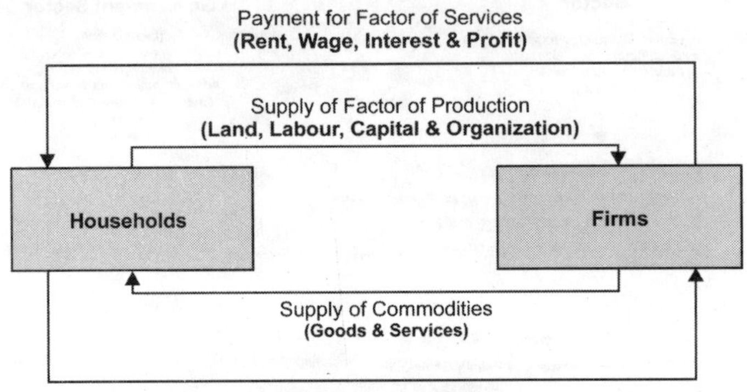

Simple Explanation through Steps

1. The public owns the factors of production and provide them to producers.
2. The producers employ the factor inputs to produce output of goods and services. The consumers (public) buy those goods and services.
3. For the employment of factor services, the public receive the factor income, namely rent (for land), wages (for labour) and interest (for capital). This income flows back from the public to the business sector as consumption expenditure to buy the goods and services.
4. Thus, the flow chart consists of two segments—real flow and money flow.

The most important point to be noted for the computation of national income is that income (Y) received is equal to the consumption expenditure (C) made by the consumers.

$$Y = C$$

However, national income is the aggregate summation of income or expenditure made through these four components, consumers (C), investors (I), government (G) and foreign trade (Exports [X] – Imports [M])

$$Y = C + I + G + (X - M)$$

Methods of Calculating National Income

1. Product or Output Method:

GDP is calculated by adding the total value of the output (of goods and services) produced by all activities during any time period such as a year.

2. Income Method:

GDP is calculated by adding all the income earned by various factors of production which are engaged in the production of output.

- Wages and salaries
- Income of self-employed
- Profits and dividends of business corporations
- Interest
- Rent
- Surplus of government enterprises
- Net flow of income from abroad

3. Expenditure Method:

GDP is calculated by adding all the expenditures made in the economy.

- C = Consumption expenditures
- I = Domestic investment
- G = Government expenditures
- X = Exports of goods and services
- M = Imports of goods and services
- NR = Net income receipts from assets abroad

$$GDP = E\text{ (expenditure)} = C + I + G + (X - M)$$

Quick Formulae

- NNP = GNP – Depreciation
- NNI = NNP – Indirect Taxes
- PI = NNI – Retained Earnings, Corporate Taxes and Interest on Public Debt
- PDI = PI – Personal Taxes

where

GNP = Gross National Product

NNP = Net National Product

NNI = Net National Income

PI = Personal Income

PDI = Personal Disposable Income

Problems in Calculating National Income

1. The problem of double-counting.
2. Circulation of black money (parallel economy based on illegal transactions).
3. Non-monetized economy (transactions that occur informally, mostly in rural economies).

4. *Household Services*: The national income analysis ignores domestic work, and housekeeping and social services. Most of such valuable work rendered by our women at home does not enter our national accounting.
5. *Environmental Cost*: National income estimation does not distinguish between environmental-friendly and environmental-hazardous industries. The cost of polluting industries is not included in the estimate.

Introduction to Human Resource

3

Human Resource Management (HRM)

It is the function within an organization that focuses on recruitment, management and providing direction for the people who work in the organization.

—*Humanresource.about.com*

In simple terms: *It is the organizational function that deals with issues related to people such as compensation, hiring, performance management, organization development, safety, wellness, benefits, employee motivation, communication, administration, and training.*

Nature of HRM

1. Inherent part of the management
2. Pervasive (constant) function
3. Basic to all functional areas
4. People centered
5. Personnel activities or functions
6. Continuous process
7. Based on human relations

Objectives of HRM

- To ensure effective utilization of human resource.
- To establish and maintain an adequate organizational structure of relationships among all members of the organization.
- To generate maximum development of human resource within the organization.
- To ensure respect for all human beings by providing welfare services.
- To ensure reconciliation of individual/group goals with those of the organization by facilitating loyalty and commitment by employees.
- To identify and satisfy the needs of individuals by offering various monetary and non-monetary rewards.
- To achieve and maintain high morale among the employees within the organization.

Scope of HRM

- Employment
- Relations among departments

- Promotion and career path
- Salary
- Job evaluation and standards
- Performance measurement
- Training
- Selection of human resources
- Dismissal
- Job description

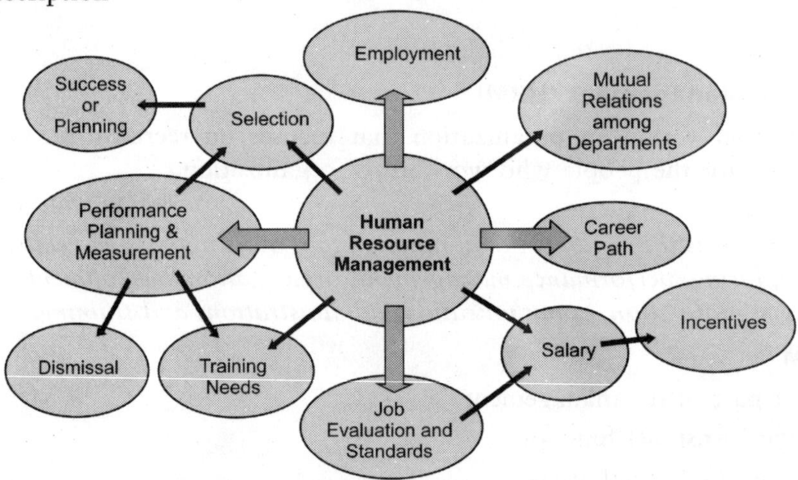

Guideline of Effective Human Resource Management

- Penetration of corporate policies, strategies and objectives into managers and employees.
- Observation of laws and regulations (labour laws and regulations), respects on labour practice.
- Projection for corporate organization (projection in employee allocation).

Functions of HRM

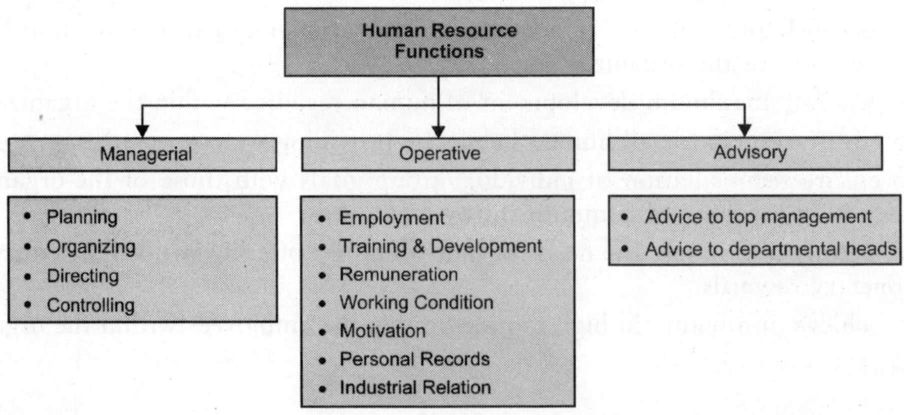

Challenges in HRM

1. Going Global
    - Globalization
        (i) The trend toward opening up foreign markets to international trade and investment.
    - Impact of globalization
        (i) "Anything, anywhere, anytime" markets.
        (ii) Partnerships with foreign firms.
        (iii) Lower trade and tariff barriers.
        (iv) Identifying capable managers and workers.
        (v) Developing foreign culture and work practice training programs.
        (vi) Adjusting compensation plans for overseas work.
2. Embracing New Technology
    - Knowledge based training.
    - Increasing demand for knowledge workers.
    - Storing and retrieving of large quantities of data.
    - Combining and reconfiguring data to create new information.
    - Institutionalization of organizational knowledge.
    - Making communications easier.
    - Ensuring lower administrative costs, increased productivity and response times.
3. Managing Change
    - Reactive change
        (i) Change that occurs after external forces have already affected performance.
    - Proactive change
        (i) Change initiated to take advantage of targeted opportunities.
        (ii) Managing Change through HR.
4. Managing Talent/Human Capital
    - Regular interaction with employees on their issues.
    - Expansion through training and development.
    - Saving talent drain.
    - Effective utilization of the right talent at the right place.
5. Responding to the Market
    - Need for creating an environment for change.
    - Development of effective leadership and communication processes.
    - Periodic reviews and modifications of administrative systems.
6. Containing Costs
    - Downsizing

(i) The planned elimination of jobs
(ii) Layoffs

- Outsourcing
  (i) Contracting outside the organization to have work done that formerly was done by internal employees.
- Off shoring
  (i) The business practice of sending jobs to other countries.
- Severance and rehiring costs.
- Accrued vacation and sick day payouts.
- Pension and benefit payoffs.
- Potential lawsuits from aggrieved workers.
- Loss of institutional memory and trust in management.
- Lack of staffers when the economy rebounds.
- Survivors who are risk-averse, paranoid, and political.

Human Resource (Personnel) Policies

In simple terms: *They lay down the decision-making criteria in the line with the overall purpose of the organization in the area of human resource management.*

Characteristics of a Policy

- It is an expression of the intentions of top management.
- It is stated in broad terms.
- It is long lasting.
- It is developed with active participation of all human resources.
- It is in writing.
- It is linked with objectives.

Difference between Policy, Procedure and Strategy

Policy	Procedure	Strategy
It is a definite course of action adopted in an effort to promote the best practice particular to desired results.	A procedure is a particular way of accomplishing something.	It is a plan or method of approach developed to successfully achieve an overall goal or objective.
A policy is a guiding principle.	A procedure is a series of steps.	
It is made to guide taking actions under situation which arise repeatedly.	It is guide to action where steps are to be taken in a chorological manner.	It is made only when there is a need to give a sharp focus on an objective.
It is type of standing plan.	It is laid down to implement some policy.	It is a single use plan.
It need not originate because of competition.		It originates due to competition.

Organization Structure

In simple terms: *It is the formal and informal framework of policies and rules, within which an organization arranges its lines of authority and communications, and allocates rights and duties.*

Line and Staff Authority

- Line Authority—Power to give orders to subordinates.
- Staff Authority—Authority to advise, but not to direct, other managers.

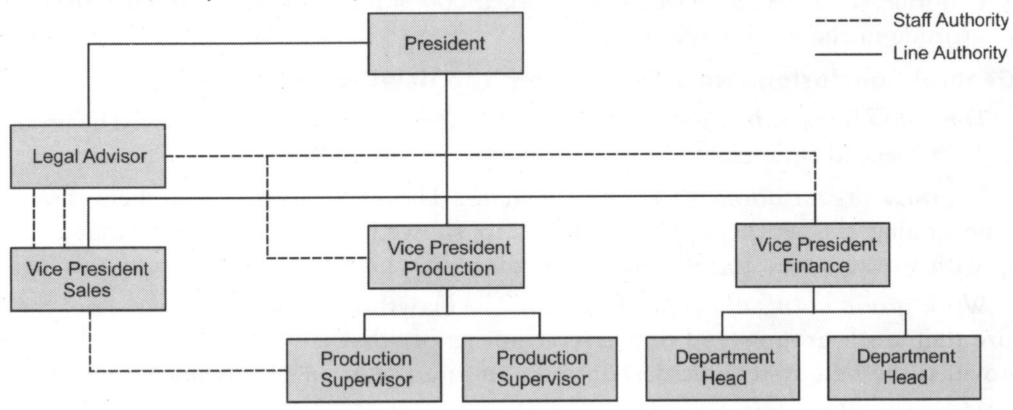

Line Authority	Staff Authority
Right to decide and to command.	Right to provide advice, assistance and information.
Contributes directly to accomplishment of goals.	Assists line in the effective accomplishment of goals.
Relatively unlimited and general.	Relatively restricted to a particular function.
Flows downward from a superior to a subordinate.	May flow in any direction depending upon the need of advice.
Possessed by generalists.	Possessed by specialists.
Creats superior-subordinate relations.	Extension of line and supports line.
Exercise control.	Investigates and reports.
Makes operating decisions.	Provides ideas for decisions.
Bears final responsibility for results.	Does not bear final responsibility.
Doing function.	Thinking function.
Provides channel of communication.	No channel of communication is created.

Human Relations Approach

In simple terms: *It pertains to motivating people in organizations in order to develop teamwork which effectively fulfils their needs and leads to achieving organizational goals.*

Hawthorne Experiment

George Elton Mayo was in charge of certain experiments on human behaviour carried out at the Hawthorne Works of the General Electric Company in Chicago between 1924 and 1927. His research findings have contributed to organization development in terms of human relations and motivation theory.

1. *Illumination Tests*: Lighting intensity was altered to examine its effect on worker productivity.

2. *Relay-Assembly Tests*: The relay-assembly tests were designed to evaluate the effect rest periods and hours of work would have on efficiency.

3. *Bank-Wiring Tests*: The purpose of the next study was to find out how payment incentives would affect group productivity.

4. *Interviewing Program*: The workers were interviewed about supervisory practices and employee morale. The results proved that upward communication in an organization creates a positive attitude in the work environment.

Four General Conclusions were Drawn from the Hawthorne Studies

1. *The aptitudes of individuals are imperfect predictors of job performance*: The productivity is strongly influenced by social factors.

2. *Informal organization affects productivity*: The Hawthorne researchers discovered a group life among the workers. The studies also showed that the relations that supervisors develop with workers tend to influence the manner in which the workers carry out directives.

3. *Work-group norms affect productivity*: The Hawthorne researchers were not the first to recognize that work groups tend to arrive at norms of what is "a fair day's work", however, they provided the best systematic description and interpretation of this phenomenon.

4. *The workplace is a social system*: The Hawthorne researchers came to view the workplace as a social system made up of interdependent parts.

Human Resource Planning/Manpower Planning

It is a process of determining manpower requirements and the means for meeting those requirements in order to carry out the integrated plan of the organization.

—*Coleman*

Benefits of Human Resource Planning

1. Enable the determination of personnel needs of an organization.
2. It is an essential component of strategic planning.
3. It helps to ascertain and identify critical shortages of skilled staff and take corrective action by timely recruitment, etc. so as to prevent production break-down or under-utilization of plant capacity.
4. An integral part of managerial succession plan by identifying and developing potential managers.
5. Enable organization to cope with changes in competitive forces, markets, technology, product, etc.
6. Enable the procurement of personnel with necessary qualification, skill knowledge, work experience and proper work attitude.
7. Involves in selection and development of employees well in advance so as to meet any contingencies.
8. Besides looking and reacting to staff deficit, manpower planning is also able to identify any surplus/redundancy, if any in an organization.

Steps in Human Resource Planning

1. Review the manpower requirements either basing on existing company's plans and conduct a forecasting of future manpower both in term of quantity and quality of staff.
2. Conduct a stock count to see assess and identify whether the human resources are being used optimally.
3. Anticipate manpower problems by comparison of current with the forecast requirements.
4. Planning the necessary programmes whether recruitment, selection, training, development, utilization, transfer, promotion, motivation and compensation to ensure that future manpower requirements of the industry are properly met.

Problems in Human Resource Planning

- Lack of fully understanding the manpower planning process by all managers.
- Need of top management is required for effective control.
- Lack of initial insufficient efforts.
- Lack of coordination with other management functions will result in failure.
- Lack of proper integration with 'organizational plans' will create discrepancies.
- Involvement of operating managers is must, without which the planning is useless.

Recruitment

In simple terms: *The process of screening, and selecting qualified people for a job at an organization.*

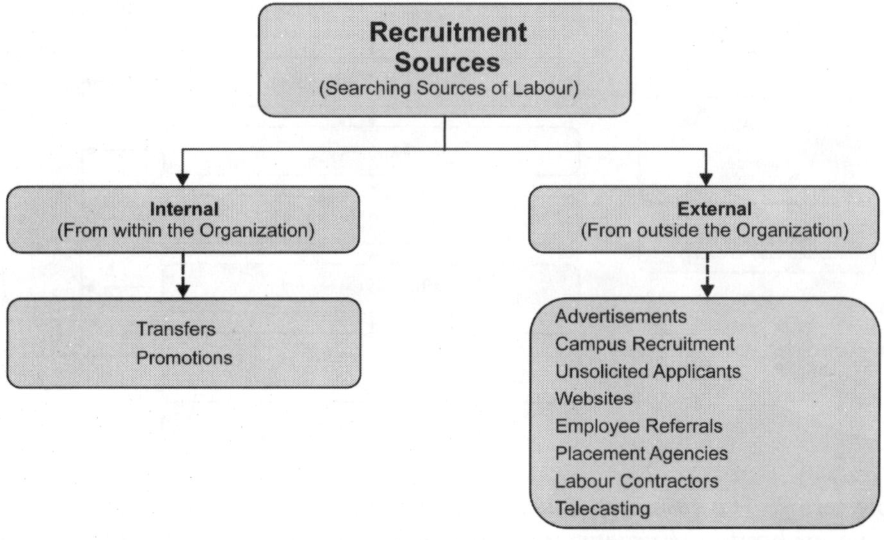

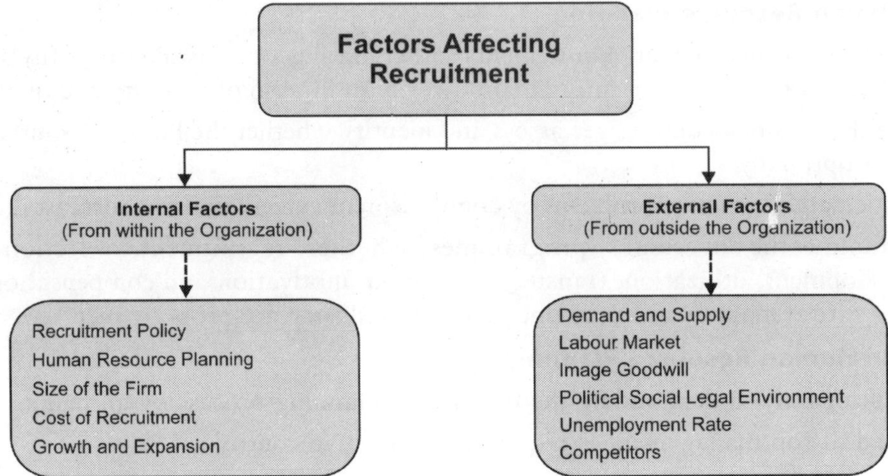

Selection

In simple terms: *It involves a series of steps by which the candidates are screened for choosing the most suitable persons for vacant posts.*

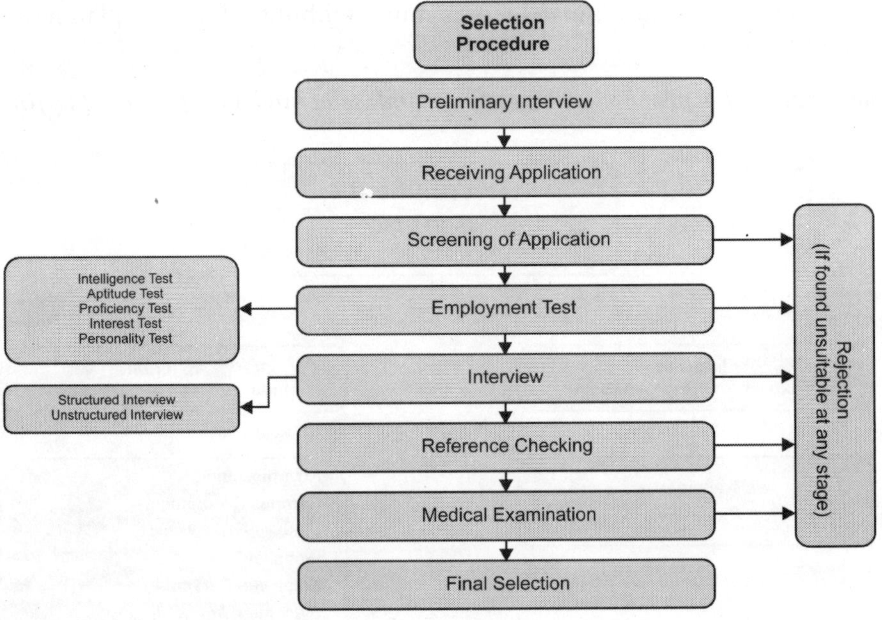

Induction

In simple terms: *The first step towards introducing the job and organization to the new recruit and him or her to the organization. It involves orientation and training of the employee in the organizational culture, and showing how he or she is interconnected to everyone else in the organization.*

Transfer

In simple terms: *It is a lateral move to a position in the same classified pay range or to a position with comparable duties and responsibilities.*

Promotion

In simple terms: *It is an appointment to a position requiring higher qualifications such as greater skill or longer experience and involving a higher level of responsibility, a higher rate of pay and a title change.*

Training

In simple terms: *It is the act of increasing the knowledge and skills of an employee for doing a particular job.*

Benefits of Training

- Building confidence in both employees and the organization.
- Reduce errors and resulting complaints.
- Reduce liability risk to the organization.
- Improve job satisfaction and motivation.
- Lesson employee conflict.
- Increase morale.
- Decrease turnover and absenteeism.

On-the-Job Training Methods

- Job instruction training
- Job rotation
- Mentoring

Off-the-Job Training Methods

- Classroom
- Group discussion
- Simulation methods
- Role-playing

Distance Learning

- Interactive video
- Web-based training
- Computer-assisted training

Evaluating the Training Program

- Participant reaction—evaluate trainee's attitudes and feelings.
- Knowledge gained in classroom—application of concepts are reflected by greater knowledge.
- Change in on-the-job behaviour—assess changed behaviour on the job.
- Measurable influence of the training on the organization—impacts the bottom line or improves productivity.

Job Analysis

In simple terms: *It is the process used for collecting information about the duties, responsibilities, necessary skills, outcomes, and work environment of a particular job.*

Essentials for Job Analysis

1. Must be for the job where selection device will be used.
2. Should be in writing.
3. Detailed analysis procedures should be used.
4. Data must be collected by knowledgeable analyst.
5. Sample size should be large and representative.
6. Must include tasks, duties, and activities.

Methods for Collecting 'Job Analysis' Information

1. *Work-oriented methods*: It can be used both work improvement, job definition and also for recruitment.

- *Structured questionnaire*: Questionnaires and checklists to organize.
- *Process analysis*: Breaking down the activities.
- *Observation*: Researcher just watches what is done.
- *Self-reports*: The incumbent reports what happens using diaries and logs.
- *Participation*: The researcher does the job.

2. *Worker-oriented methods*: Worker-oriented methods are focused on the person and their experience and perception.

- *Interview*: The incumbent is questioned about the job.
  - (a) Must have been frequently used.
  - (b) Interviews should be with incumbents and supervisors.
  - (c) Assumes thorough familiarity with the job.
  - (d) It can have either 'structured' or 'unstructured' format.
  - (e) It can be used to identify critical job tasks.
- *Limitations*:
  - (f) Heavily dependent on interviewing ability.
  - (g) Takes a lot of time and may not be cost efficient in all cases.
  - (h) A lot of cross verification may be required to get a clear picture.
  - (i) Cannot be relied on as the only source of information.
- *Critical Incident Technique*: Finding successful and unsuccessful behaviours in key incidents.
- *Repertory Grid*: Finding similarities and differences and hence constructs.

Job Description

In simple terms: *Broad, general, and written statement of a specific job, based on the findings of a job analysis. It generally includes duties, purpose, responsibilities, scope, and working conditions of a job along with the job's title, and the name or designation of the person to whom the employee reports. Job description usually forms the basis of job specification.*

Job Design

In simple terms: *Work arrangement (or rearrangement) aimed at reducing or overcoming job dissatisfaction and employee alienation arising from repetitive and mechanistic tasks.*

Through job design, an organization tries to raise productivity levels by offering non-monetary rewards such as greater satisfaction from a sense of personal achievement in meeting the increased challenge and responsibility of one's work.

Techniques in Job Designing

1. *Job Enlargement*: A technique in which the number of tasks associated with a job is increased (and appropriate training provided) to add greater variety to activities, thus reducing monotony. It is a horizontal restructuring method in that the job is enlarged by adding related tasks. Job enlargement may also result in greater workforce flexibility.

2. *Job Enrichment*: A technique that adds new sources of job satisfaction by increasing the level of responsibility of the employee. It is a vertical restructuring method that gives the employee additional authority, autonomy, and control over the way the job is accomplished, also called job enhancement or vertical job expansion.

3. *Job Rotation*: A technique in which employees are moved between two or more jobs in a planned manner. The objective is to expose the employees to different experiences and wider variety of skills to enhance job satisfaction and to cross-train them.

4. *Job Simplification*: A technique in which jobs are broken into relatively simple tasks. It aims at greater productivity through reduced application of mental and/or physical effort. See also time and motion study.

Compensation

In simple terms: *It refers to a wide range of financial and non-financial rewards to the employees for their services rendered to the organization.*

Elements of Compensation

- *Base Pay*: Non-discretionary compensation that does not regularly vary according to performance or results achieved.
- *Variable Pay*: Dependent on discretion, performance or results achieved.

Factors Affecting Wage/Compensation

- Demand for Supply of Labour
- Ability to Pay
- Cost of Living
- Productivity of Workers
- Labour Unions
- Government Policies
- Prevailing Wage Rates.

Job Evaluation

In simple terms: *A technique that strives to provide a systematic, rational, and consistent approach to defining the relative worth of jobs within an organization.*

Wage Determination

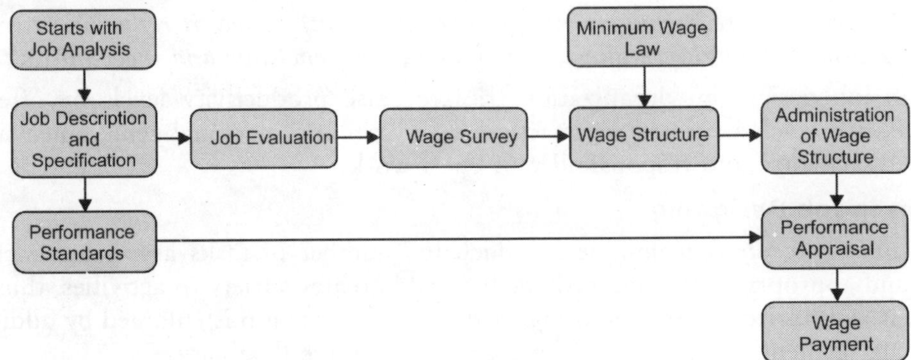

Methods of Wage Payment

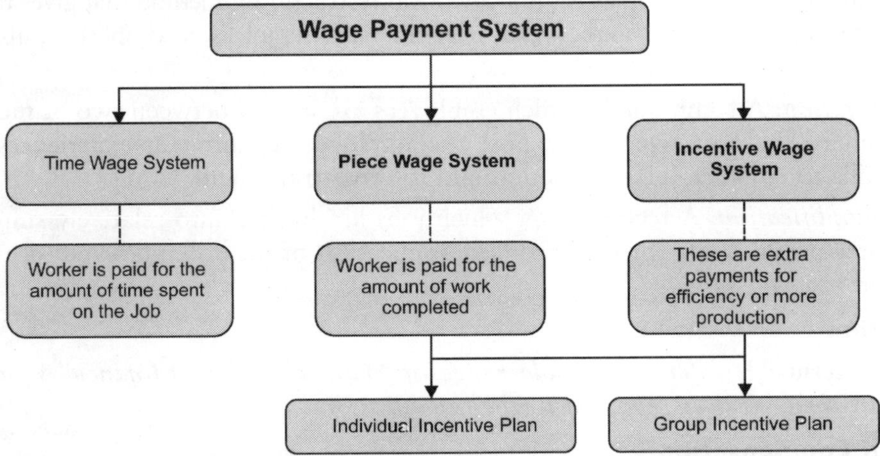

Formulae

- Time Wage System = Number of Working Hours × Rate per Hour
- Piece Wage System = Number of Units Produces × Rate per Unit

Employee Stock Option

Under this system, the employees are allotted company's shares (also known as sweet equity) below the market price.

Features of Employee Stock Option

1. Voluntary in Nature.
2. Stocks are offered below the market price.
3. Intended to hold talented employees.
4. It makes the employees a part owner of the company.
5. Stocks are held in trust until the employee chooses to withdraw or leave the company.

Performance Appraisal

In simple terms: *It is the process of obtaining, analyzing and recording information about the relative worth of an employee.*

The focus of the performance appraisal is measuring and improving the actual performance of the employee and also the future potential of the employee.

Objectives of Performance Appraisal

- To review the performance of the employees over a given period of time.
- To judge the gap between the actual and the desired performance.
- To diagnose the strengths and weaknesses of the individuals so as to identify the training and development needs of the future.
- To provide feedback to the employees regarding their past performance.
- To provide clarity of the expectations and responsibilities of the functions to be performed by the employees.
- To reduce the grievances of the employees.
- To judge the effectiveness of the other human resource functions of the organization such as recruitment, selection, training and development.
- To help the management in exercising organizational control.

What is to be Measured?

Technical Attributes

1. Knowledge and application
2. Achievement of targets
3. Other quantifiable results

Soft Skills

1. Leadership and goal clarity
2. Relationship management
3. Communication

Personal Traits

1. Honesty
2. Integrity
3. Sincerity
4. Morality
5. Ethical standing

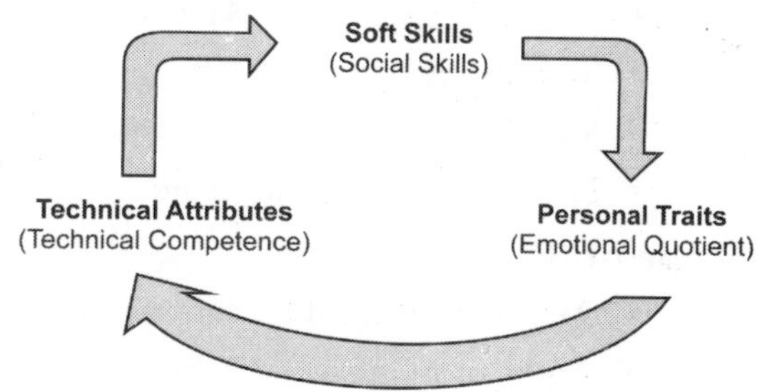

Appraisal Methods

1. *Encourage Discussion*: Employees are likely to feel more satisfied with their appraisal result if they have the chance to talk freely and discuss their performance.

2. *Constructive Intention*: It is very important that employees recognize that negative appraisal feedback is provided with a constructive intention, i.e. to help them overcome present

difficulties and to improve their future performance.

3. *Set Performance Goals*: Goal-setting is an important element in employee motivation. Goals can stimulate employee effort, focus attention, increase persistence, and encourage employees to find new and better ways to work.

4. *Appraiser Credibility*: It is important that the appraiser (usually the employee's supervisor) be well-informed and realistic.

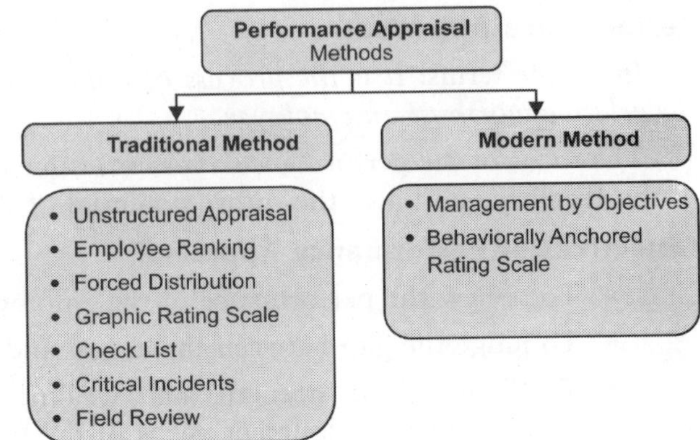

Human Resource Audit

In simple terms: *It refers to an examination and evaluation of personnel policies, procedures and practices to determine the effectiveness of human resource management.*

Benefits of Human Resource (HR) Audit

- It helps to find out the proper contribution of the HR department towards the organization.
- Reduce the HR cost.
- Motivation of the HR staff.
- Identification of problems and resolutions for them.
- Provides timely legal requirement.
- Sound Performance Appraisal Systems.
- Systematic job analysis.
- Smooth adoption of the changing mindset.
- Development of the professional image of the HR department of the organization.

Scope of HR Audit

- Audit of all the HR functions.
- Audit of managerial compliance of personnel policies, procedures and legal provisions.
- Audit of corporate strategy regarding HR planning, staffing, IRs, remuneration and other HR activities.
- Audit of the HR climate on employee motivation, morale and job satisfaction.

Aspects of HR Audit

- Personal policy.
- Human resource planning.
- Recruitment, selection and placement.
- Human resource training development.
- Transfers and promotions.
- Performance appraisal reports.

- Employee relations.
- Communications, suggestion schemes, areas of participation.
- Compensation, rewards, benefits and services.
- Welfare activities undertaking by the management.

Method of HR Audit

- Interviewing key staff.
- Review relevant documentation.
- Help you complete a comprehensive questionnaire.
- Compile data and prepare and customized written report.
- Make specific recommendations to improve the efficiency and performance of your HR function.

Morale and Productivity

Requirements for Effective Morale Building for Efficient Performance

- Goals must be specific.
- Goals must be challenging.
- Workers must have necessary ability.
- Feedback is provided.
- Rewards are clearly understood and provided.
- Management supports goal attainment.
- Provision of necessary time and resources.
- Goals are internalized and accepted by employees.

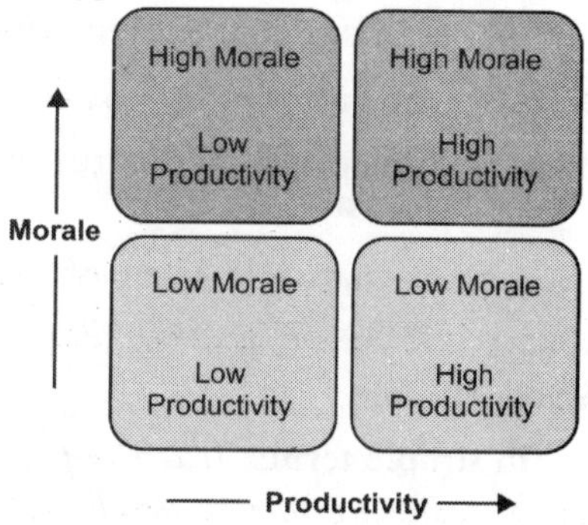

High Morale Low Productivity | High Morale High Productivity
Low Morale Low Productivity | Low Morale High Productivity
Morale
Productivity

Industrial Psychology

In simple terms: *It is the branch of applied psychology that is concerned with efficient management of an industrial labour force and especially with problems encountered by workers.*

Contemporary Labour Problems

Labour Turnover

In simple terms: *It refers to the movement of employees in and out of a business. However, the term is commonly used to refer only to 'wastage' or the number of employees leaving.*

Labour Turnover Measurement

The simplest measure involves calculating the number of leavers in a period (usually a year) as a percentage of the number employed during the same period. This is known as the "separation rate".

Formula: Number of Leavers/Average Number Employed × 100

Causes of Labour Turnover

- Inadequate wage levels leading to employees moving to competitors.
- Poor morale and low levels of motivation within the workforce.
- Recruiting and selecting the wrong employees in the first place, meaning they leave to seek more suitable employment.
- A buoyant local labour market offering more (and perhaps more attractive) opportunities to employees.

Costs of Labour Turnover

- Additional recruitment costs.
- Lost production costs.
- Increased costs of training replacement employees.
- Loss of know-how and customer goodwill.
- Potential loss of sales (e.g. if there is high turnover amongst the sales force).
- Damage that may be done to morale and productivity (an intangible cost).

Benefits of Labour Turnover

- Sometimes labour turnover is important to bring new ideas, skills and enthusiasm to the labour force.
- A "natural" level of labour turnover can be a way in which a business can slowly reduce its workforce.

Absenteeism

In simple terms: *It is the problem of employees taking short-term, unauthorized leave from work, resulting in lost productivity and increased costs.*

Notable Hidden Cost Factors Associated with Absenteeism

- Lost productivity of the absent employee.
- Overtime for other employees to fill in.
- Decreased overall productivity of those employees.
- Any temporary help costs incurred.
- Possible loss of business or dissatisfied customers.
- Problems with employee morale.

Employee Health, Safety and Security

For smooth functioning of an organization, the employer has to ensure safety and security of his employees. It is the responsibility of the employers to provide a safe and healthful workplace for their employees.

- Health not only includes physical well-being, but also emotional and mental well-being.
- Safety includes protecting against the risk of accidents caused due to machinery, fire or diseases.
- Security includes protecting facilities and equipments from unauthorized access and usage.

Direct Cost Saving Benefits to the Organization

1. Lower workers' compensation insurance costs.
2. Reduced medical expenditures.
3. Smaller expenditures for return-to-work programs.
4. Fewer faulty products.
5. Lower costs for job accommodations for injured workers.
6. Less money spent for overtime benefits.

Indirect Cost Saving Benefits to the Organization

1. Increased productivity.
2. Higher quality products.
3. Increased morale.
4. Better labour/management relations.
5. Reduced turnover.
6. Better use of human resources.

Four Basic Elements to All Good Safety and Health Programs

1. *Management Commitment and Employee Involvement*: The manager or management team leads the way, by setting policy, assigning and supporting responsibility, setting an example and involving employees.

2. *Worksite Analysis*: The worksite is continually analyzed to identify all existing and potential hazards.

3. *Hazard Prevention and Control*: Methods to prevent or control existing or potential hazards are put in place and maintained.

4. *Training for Employees, Supervisors and Managers*: Managers, supervisors and employees are trained to understand and deal with worksite hazards.

Human Resource Development

In simple terms: *Human Resource Development is the framework for helping employees develops their personal and organizational skills, knowledge, and abilities.*

It includes

- Employee training.
- Employee career development.
- Performance management and development.
- Coaching.
- Key employee identification.
- Tuition assistance.
- Organization development.

The focus of all aspects of Human Resource Development is on developing the most superior workforce so that the organization and individual employees can achieve their work goals in service to customers.

Quality Circle

In simple terms: *A group of employees who perform similar duties and meet at periodic intervals, often with management, to discuss work-related issues and to offer suggestions and ideas for improvements, as in production methods or quality control.*

Characteristics of Quality Circle

- Voluntary group.
- Set rules and priorities.
- Decisions made by consensus.
- Use of organized approaches to problem-solving.

How does it Work?

- All members of a circle need to receive training.
- Members need to be authorized.
- Members need to have the support of senior management.

Benefits of Quality Circle

- Increase productivity.
- Improve quality.
- Boost employee morale.

Total Quality Management (TQM)

In simple terms: *It is a continuous customer-centered employee driven improvement.*

Basically, it is a process of achieving best possible outcomes from the inputs, by using them effectively and efficiently in order to deliver best value for the customer, while achieving long-term objectives of the organization.

Characteristics of TQM

- It is a customer focused approach.
- It aims at satisfying the customer or delighting them.
- It provides best quality product at lowest possible price.
- It is company wide strategy.
- It involves everyone in the organization.
- It focuses on prevention of defects and targets zero defects.
- It is methodical.
- It operates based on information.

TQM Process Steps

Industrial Relation

In simple terms: *Relations between the management of an industrial enterprise and its employees.*

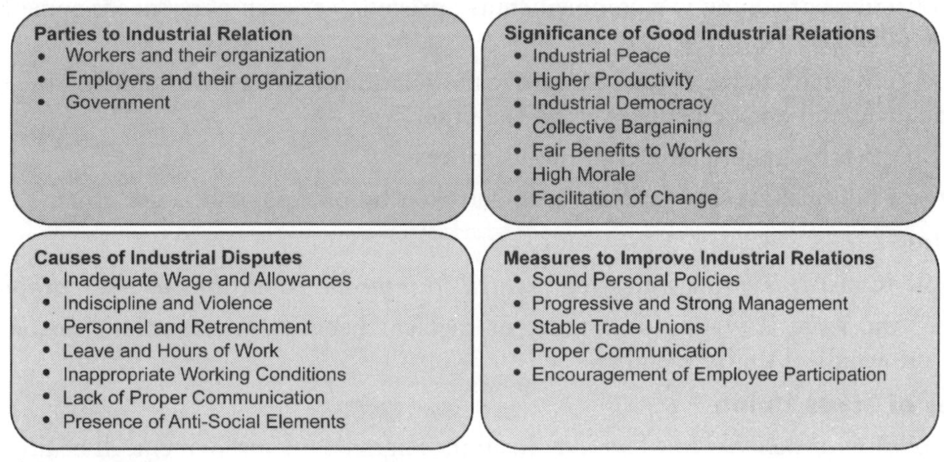

Industrial Democracy

In simple terms: *Participation of employees' representatives from all or most levels of an industrial organization in its decision-making process.*

Benefits of Industrial Democracy

- Less industrial disputes resulting from better communication at workplace.
- Improved decision-making processes resulting in higher quality decisions.
- Increased creativity, enthusiasm and commitment to corporate objectives.
- Lowered stress and increased well-being.
- Better use of time and resources.

- Improved productivity including service delivery.
- Increased job satisfaction resulting in reduced absenteeism.
- Improved personal fulfillment and self-esteem.

Forms of Industrial Democracy

1. Representative
2. Participative

Collective Bargaining

In simple terms: *A method of negotiation in which employees use authorized union representatives to assist them.*

Characteristics of Collective Bargaining

- It is a group process.
- Negotiations form an important aspect of the process of collective bargaining.
- Collective bargaining is a formalized process by which employers and independent trade unions negotiate.
- Collective bargaining is a bipartite process in the sense that it consists of a number of steps.
- Collective bargaining is a complementary process, i.e. each party needs something that the other party has.
- Collective bargaining tends to improve the relations between workers and the union on the one hand and the employer on the other.
- Collective bargaining is a continuous process.
- It is a political activity frequently undertaken by professional negotiators.

Trade Union

In simple terms: *It is an organization created to improve conditions in the workplace.*

Whether the issue is wages, sick time, or medical benefits, trade unions negotiate with employers on behalf of union members.

Objectives of Trade Union

- *Provision of Benefits to Members*: Insurance against unemployment, ill health, old age, funeral expenses, provision of professional training, legal advice and representation for members.
- *Collective Bargaining*: Where trade unions are able to operate openly and are recognized by employers, they may negotiate with employers over wages and working conditions.
- *Industrial Action*: Trade unions may enforce strikes or resistance to lockouts in furtherance of particular goals.
- *Political Activity*: Trade unions may promote legislation favourable to the interests of their members or workers as a whole.

Introduction to Business Management (Concepts and Practices)

4

Organization

It is a system of consciously coordinated activities of two or more persons.

—*Chester Bernard*

In simple terms: *An organization can be expressed as a collection of individuals deliberately structured within identifiable boundaries to achieve pre-determined goals.*

Salient Features of an Organization

1. Organizations are social entities.
2. All organizations have a structure.
3. Organizations are designed to achieve specific goals.
4. Organizations have identifiable boundaries.
5. Organizations exist in a relatively permanent basis.
6. All formal organizations use specific knowledge (or technology) to perform work-related activities.

Organizational Goals

As per Henry Minztberg, different classifications of organizational goals are as under:

- *System Goals*: There are four system goals: survival, efficiency, control and growth.
- *Formal Goals*: They are used by managers to tell everyone what they are doing.
- *Ideological Goals*: These goals are what the people within the organization believe in.
- *Shared Personal Goals*: Goals that people within the organization achieve for their mutual benefit together.

Organizational Resources

The different resources an organization uses to achieve goals are:

- Human resources.
- Financial resources.
- Physical resource.
- Information resources.

Organizational Performance

The most common ways are in terms of efficiency or effectiveness. According to Richard Daft, "Performance is the attainment of organizational goals by using resources in an efficient and effective manner".

Effectiveness and efficiency are viewed as subcomponents of performance. As per Peter Drucker, efficiency means "doing things right" and effectiveness means "doing the right things".

In simple terms: *Organizational efficiency refers to the amount of resources used to achieve an organizational goal.*

A Framework for Performance

- Performance is not single standard, but consists of multiple criteria.
- The level of analysis of performance ranges from the individual employee to the user of the organization's products and services, and on to society in general.
- The focus of performance can concern maintenance, improvement, and developmental goals.
- The time frame for performance, from short-term to long-term, must be established.
- How performance will be measured, ranging from quantitative/objective to qualitative/subjective measures should be considered.

Business Management

Business Management is simply the act of getting people together to achieve desired goals.

–Mary Parker Follett

In simple words: *The art of getting things done through people.*

According to Henri Fayol, management comprises the following:

- *Planning*: Deciding what needs to happen in the future.
- *Organizing*: Making optimum use of the resources required to enable the successful carrying out of plans.
- *Leading*: Determining what needs to be done in a situation and getting people to do it.
- *Coordinating*: Bridging the gaps and building synergies by synchronization of efforts.
- *Controlling*: Checking progress against plans, which may need modification accordingly.
- *Staffing*: Job analyzing, recruitment and hiring individuals for appropriate responsibilities.
- *Motivating*: The process of stimulating an individual to take action that will achieve a desired goal.

The Scope of Management

Management is needed in all types of organized activities. Moreover, management principles are applicable to all types of organizations, including profit-seeking organizations (industrial firms, banks, insurance companies, small business, etc.) and not-for-profit organizations (governmental organizations, health care organizations, educations organizations, churches, etc.).

Management is also universal because it uses a systematic body of knowledge including economics, sociology, and laws. This knowledge can be applied to all organizations, whether business, or government, or religious, and they are applicable at all levels of management in same organizations.

Manager

In simple terms: *A manager is someone who plans, organizes, leads, and controls human, financial, physical, and information resources.*

Managerial Roles

According to Mintzberg, "diverse manager activities can be organized into ten roles". These ten kinds of roles can be divided into three categories:

1. Interpersonal

- *The Figurehead Role*: Every manager must perform some duties of a ceremonial nature (e.g. the president greets the touring dignitaries, the sales manager takes an important customer to lunch). These activities are important to the smooth functioning of an organization.
- *The Leader Role*: This role involves direct leadership function (e.g. hiring and training the staff). The leader role encompasses relationships with subordinates, including motivation, communication, and influence.
- *The Liaison Role*: Making contacts inside and outside the organization (e.g. contacts with subordinates, clients, business associates, government, and trade organization officials, etc.).

2. Informational

- *The Monitor Role*: Seeking current information from many sources (e.g. scanning environment for information, interaction with liaison contacts and subordinates and receives unsolicited information).
- *The Disseminator Role*: Passing information to other, both inside and outside the organization.
- *The Spokesperson Role*: Sending selected information to people outside the organization about company policies, requirements, actions or future plans.

3. Decisional

- *The Entrepreneur Role*: Search for improvement in business to adopt according to the environment.
- *The Disturbance Handler Role*: Responding to high-pressure disturbances (e.g. resolving conflicts among subordinates or between related departments).
- *The Resource Allocator Role*: Allocate people, budget, equipment, time and other resources to attain desired outcomes.
- *The Negotiator Role*: The negotiations are duties of the manager's job. These activities involve formal negotiations and bargaining to attain outcomes for the manager's unit responsibility.

Management Skills

- *Conceptual Skills*: Cognitive ability to see the organization as a whole and the relationship among its parts. The mental capacity to understand how various functions of the organization complement one another, how the organization relates to its environment, and how changes in one part of the organization affect the rest of the organization.

- *Human Skills*: The ability to communicate with, understand and motivate individuals and groups.
- *Technical Skills*: Skills necessary to achieve specialized activities (e.g. engineering, programming and accounting, etc.).
- *Diagnostic Skills*: The ability to determine, by analysis and examination, the nature of a particular condition.
- *Political Skills*: The ability to acquire the power necessary to reach objectives and to prevent others from taking power.

Management: Is it Science or Art?

It is both. Managing, like all other practices (e.g. music composition, medicine, or even tennis) is an art. To manage effectively, people must have not only the necessary abilities to lead but also a set of critical skills acquired through time, experience, and practice.

On the other hand, the organized knowledge underlying the practice may be referred to as a science. In a variety of situations, managers need economics, sociology, mathematics, political science, psychology, and political science for assistance and guidance.

School of Management Thought

The history of management theories helps us in organizing information and providing a systematic framework for action.

"The most effective formal organization in the history of western civilization has been the Roman Catholic Church".

—Harold Koontz and Cyril O'Donnell

However, management gained in importance, as mankind progressed and moved into the Industrial Revolution era.

Difference between Administration and Management

Description	Administration	Management
Nature of work	Concerned about the determination of objectives and major policies of an organization.	It puts into action the policies and plans laid down by the administration.
Type of function	It is a determinative function.	It is an executive function.
Scope	It takes major decisions of an enterprise as a whole.	It takes decisions within the framework set by the administration.
Level of authority	It is a top-level activity.	It is a middle-level activity.
Nature of status	It consists of owners who invest capital in and receive profits from an enterprise.	It is a group of managerial personnel who use their specialized knowledge to fulfill the objectives of an enterprise.
Nature of usage	It is popular with government, military, educational, and religious organizations.	It is used in business enterprises.
Decision making	Its decisions are influenced by public opinion, government policies, social, and religious factors.	Its decisions are influenced by the values, opinions, and beliefs of the managers.
Main functions	Planning and organizing functions are involved in it.	Motivating and controlling functions are involved in it.
Abilities	It needs administrative rather than technical abilities.	It requires technical activities.

Difference between Human Relation and Scientific Management

Human Relations Management	Scientific Management
Principles are not universal.	Principles are universally applicable.
The focus is on people.	The focus is on machines.
There is no single best way of doing things.	There is one best way of doing things.
Group dynamics, motivation and job satisfaction.	Time and motion studies, functional foremanship and wage incentives.
Application of knowledge derived from behavioral science.	Application of knowledge derived from physical science.
Improvement in interpersonal relations.	Improvement in productivity.

Approaches to Management

- *The Classical Approach*: Emerged during the nineteenth and early twentieth centuries. It includes two different areas:
  1. Lower-level Management Analysis (Scientific Management)
     - (a) Development of a scientific method for each element of a worker's job to replace rules of thumb.
     - (b) Job specialization to be a part of each job.
     - (c) Ensuring proper selection, training, and development of workers.
     - (d) Planning and scheduling of the work.
     - (e) Laying standards with respect to methods and time for each task.
     - (f) Wage incentives to be an integral part of each job.
  2. Comprehensive Analysis of Management (Administrative Theory)

     Fourteen General Principles (Developed by Fayol) are as under:
     - (a) *Division of Labor*: Specialization of labour results in increased productivity.
     - (b) *Authority*: The right to give orders and the power to exact obedience to carry out managerial responsibilities.
     - (c) *Discipline*: Employees must respect the rules that govern the organization.
     - (d) *Unity of Command*: Employees should receive orders from only one superior.
     - (e) *Unity of Direction*: Each group of activities in an organization should be grouped together under one head and one plan.
     - (f) *Subordination of Individual Interests to the General Interest*: The interests of one person should not be placed before the interests of the organization as a whole.
     - (g) *Remuneration*: Compensation should be based on systematic attempt to reward good performance.
     - (h) *Centralization*: The degree to which centralization or decentralization should be adopted depends on the specific organization, but managers should retain final responsibility to do the tasks successfully.
     - (i) *Scalar Chain*: A chain of authority should extend from the top to the bottom of the organization.

(j) *Order*: Human and material resources must be in the right place at the right time.

(k) *Equity*: Employees should be treated as equally as possible.

(l) *Stability of Personnel*: Successful firms usually had a stable group of employees.

(m) *Initiative*: Employees should have the freedom to take initiative.

(n) *Esprit de corps*: Managers should encourage a sense of unity of effort through harmony of interests.

- *The Behavioral Approach*: It includes motivation, communication, leadership, organizational politics, and employee behaviour.

  It has two branches:

  (a) The Human Relations Approach

  (b) The Behavioral Science Approach.

- *Contingency Approach*: It tells us that the effectiveness of various managerial practices, styles, techniques, and functions vary according to the particular circumstances of the situation. It basically asserts that when managers make a decision, they must take into account all aspects of the current situation and act on those aspects that are important to the situation at hand.

- *Systems Approach*: It emerged during 19th and 20th centuries. The systems approach emerged as scientists and philosophers identified common themes in the approach to managing and organizing complex systems.

  The systems approach considers two basic components: Elements and Processes. Elements are measurable things that can be linked together, while Processes change elements from one form to another. Systemic management has to achieve a sustainable balance between steering variables.

- *The Human Relations Movement*: The Harvard researches suggested that the way people were treated had an important impact on performance; individual and social processes played a major role in shaping worker attitudes and behaviour. Therefore, management must recognize the importance worker's needs for recognition and social satisfaction.

Hawthorne Experiment

George Elton Mayo was in charge of certain experiments on human behaviour carried out at the Hawthorne Works of the General Electric Company in Chicago between 1924 and 1927.

Flowing from the findings of these investigations he came to certain conclusions as follows:

1. Work is a group activity.

2. The social world of the adult is primarily patterned about work activity.

3. The need for recognition, security and sense of belonging is more important in determining worker's morale and productivity than the physical conditions under which he works.

4. A complaint is not necessarily an objective recital of facts; it is commonly a symptom manifesting disturbance of an individual's status position.

5. The worker is a person whose attitudes and effectiveness are conditioned by social demands from both inside and outside the work plant.

6. Informal groups within the work plant exercise strong social controls over the work habits and attitudes of the individual worker.

7. The change from an established society in home to an adaptive society in the work plant resulting from the use of new techniques tends continually to disrupt the social organization of a work plant and industry generally.

8. Group collaboration does not occur by accident; it must be planned and developed. If group collaboration is achieved the human relations within a work plant may reach a cohesion which resists the disrupting effects of adaptive society.

- *The Management Science School*: The management science school provides managers with a scientific basis for solving problems and making decisions.

Planning

In simple terms: *Formulation of objectives, policies, procedure, rules, programs and budgets to achieve specified goals.*

It is the process of setting goals, developing strategies, and outlining tasks and schedules to achieve the goals.

Characteristics of Planning

1. It is goal-oriented
2. It is basic to all managerial functions
3. Pervasive
4. Interdependent process
5. Future-oriented
6. Forecasting integral to planning
7. Continuous process
8. Intellectual process
9. Integrating process
10. Planning and control are inseparable
11. Choice among alternative courses of action
12. Flexible process.

Limitations of Planning

1. Dependent on information that may be inaccurate.
2. Involves time and cost.
3. It does not posses in-built flexibility.
4. May have to face resistance at times by other.

5. It has to be changed in accordance with the situation.
6. It may not be well coordinated.
7. It may not be balanced, that is, too much emphasis is placed on a single aspect.

These reasons also result in failure of a Plan.

Characteristics of Effective Planning

1. Laying clear-cut objectives.
2. Making it simple and easily understandable.
3. Making it flexible and adoptable.
4. Facilitating participation at organizational level.
5. Gaining top management support.
6. Ensuring balanced in all respects along with reasonable comprehensiveness.
7. Preparation with proper consultation of the concerned person.
8. Developing a suitable management information system.
9. Ensuring effective communication.
10. Encouraging an open system approach.
11. Conducting cost benefit analysis.
12. Periodic reviews.

Planning Principles

1. *Comprehensive*: All significant options and impacts are considered.
2. *Efficient*: The process should not waste time or money.
3. *Inclusive*: People affected by the plan have opportunities to be involved.
4. *Informative*: Results are understood by stakeholders (people affected by a decision).
5. *Integrated*: Individual, short-term decisions should support strategic, long-term goals.
6. *Logical:* Each step leads to the next.
7. *Transparent:* Everybody involved understands how the process operates.

Steps in Planning

1. *Analyzing Environment*: SWOT (Strengths Weaknesses Opportunities and Threats) analysis.

2. *Establishing Objectives or Goals*: Identified and defined goals.

3. *Seeking Necessary Information*: All relevant data and facts must be collected from internal and external sources.

4. Necessary modifications in objective and goals to be made if required.

5. *Establishing the Planning Premises*: In order to develop consistent and coordinate plans, it is necessary that planning is based upon carefully considered assumption and predictions.

6. *Identifying the Alternative Course of Action*: After established the goals or objectives and taking other related steps, feasible alternative programs or course of action are to be searched out.

7. *Evaluating the Alternatives*: Problems consequences of each alternative course of action in terms of its pros and cons are assessed.

8. *Selecting the Alternative or Course of Action*: The alternative which appears to be most feasible and conducive to the accomplishment of company's objective, is to be selected.

Types of Planning

1. *Strategic Planning*: It is an organization's process of defining its strategy, or direction, and making decisions on allocating its resources to pursue this strategy, including its capital and people.

2. *Corporate Planning*: The process of drawing up detailed action plans to achieve an organization's goals and objectives, taking into account the resources of the organization and the environment within which it operates. Corporate planning represents a formal, structured approach to achieving objectives and to implementing the corporate strategy of an organization.

3. *Operational Plan*: A highly detailed plan formulated generally by junior or departmental managers to achieve tactical objectives.

Decision Making

In simple terms: *It is an outcome of mental processes (cognitive process), which leads to the selection of a course of action among several alternatives.*

Decision Levels

1. *Strategic Decisions*: They are the highest level. Here a decision concerns general direction, long-term goals, philosophies and values. These decisions are the least structured and most imaginative; they are the most risky and of the most uncertain outcome, partly because they reach so far into the future and partly because they are of such importance.

2. *Tactical Decisions*: They support strategic decisions. They tend to be medium range, medium significance, with moderate consequences.

3. *Operational Decisions*: These are every day decisions and are used to support tactical decisions. They are often made with little thought and are structured. Their impact is immediate, short term, short range, and usually low cost.

Steps in Decision Making

1. *Defining a Decision*: Recognition of a problem arises and a diagnosis is made.

2. *Analyzing a Decision*: Analyze the decision by asking the questions: what is the decision for, what will it change, what it will achieve, and whom it will affect?

3. *Reviewing Factors*: Review the different factors which affect a situation.

4. *Analyzing Possible Course of Action*: Analyze all the possible alternatives after having examined all the relevant factors.

5. *Choosing the Best Alternatives*: A particular course of action is selected from among those which are available. When the mind has carried out its calculations, it offers the decision.

6. *Implementing Decision*: Put into action. The process of decision is not complete until it is implemented and we have learnt to live with the consequences.

7. *Evaluating Decision*: The last step in decision making is the evaluation of the decision. Sometimes, there is vigorous criticism of the decision that has been made. The manager should proposed changes and their consequences.

Rational Decision Making

It involves a cognitive process where each step follows in a logical order from the one before. It is based on thinking through and weighing up the alternatives to come up with the best potential result.

Steps in a Rational Decision Making Model

1. Define the situation/decision to be made.
2. Identify the important criteria for the process and the result.
3. Consider all possible solutions.
4. Calculate the consequences of these solutions versus the likelihood of satisfying the criteria.
5. Choose the best option.

Bounded Rationality

The term is thought to have been coined by Herbert Simon. In Models of Man, Herbert Simon points out that most people are only partly rational, and are in fact emotional/irrational in the remaining part of their actions.

Reasons

1. Inadequate goal formulation.
2. Vaguely define problems.
3. Imperfect knowledge.
4. Limited time and resources.
5. Power politics.
6. Environmental dynamics.

Management by Objectives (MBO)

In simple terms: *It is a process of agreeing upon objectives within an organization so that management and employees agree to the objectives and understand what they are in the organization.*

Objectives for MBO

SMART (Specific, Measurable, Achievable, Relevant and Time-Specific)

Limitations of MBO

1. Goal setting problem.
2. Time consuming.
3. Increased paperwork.
4. Pressure oriented.
5. Undermining leadership.
6. Participation problem.
7. Inflexibility.

Corporate Planning

In simple terms: *It is the process of drawing up detailed action plans to achieve an organization's goals and objectives, taking into account the resources of the organization and the environment within which it operates.*

Determinants of Corporate Planning

1. Size of the firm.
2. Degree of diversification.
3. Complexity of business.
4. Management attitude.
5. Planning skills.
6. Ownership patterns.
7. Market dynamics.
8. Nature of demand.
9. Time lag.

Steps in Corporate Planning

1. Environmental Analysis/Market Situation Analysis.
2. Corporate Appraisal (SWOT Analysis).

Environmental Analysis

In simple terms: *Environmental analysis is the study of the organizational environment to identify environmental factors that can significantly influence organizational operations.*

Objectives of Environmental Analysis

1. A basic understanding of the situation both inside and outside the organization.
2. To increase the probability of succeeding the organizational strategies.

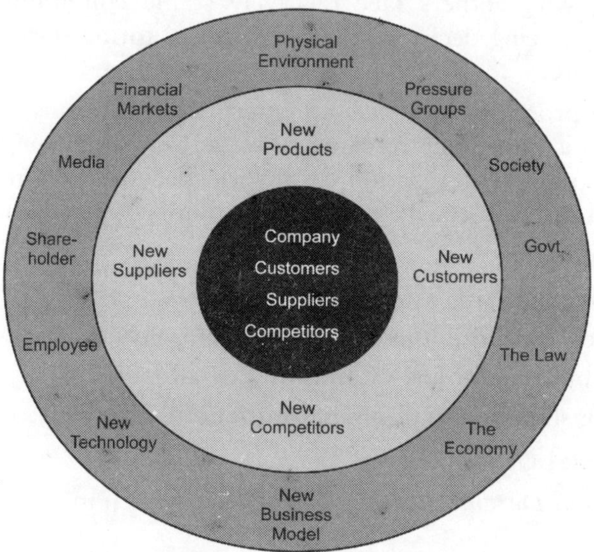

Organizing

In simple terms: *Assembling required resources to attain organizational objectives.*

It is the activity of designing, structuring, arranging, and rearranging the components of an organization's internal environment that creates the socio-technical systems that will achieve the organization's goals.

Key Features of Organizing

1. Common purpose
2. Division of labour
3. Authority structure
4. People
5. Communication
6. Coordination
7. Resources
8. Environment
9. Rules and regulation.

Factors of Organizing

1. *Strategy*: Managers organize in order to achieve the objectives of the enterprise for which they work. Thus, the strategy of the enterprise affects organizing decisions. Changes in strategy frequently necessitate changes in the way the enterprise is organized.

2. *Size*: Small enterprises tend to exhibit less formalization, centralization, and complexity in their organizational structure. Nevertheless, enterprises of the same size may be organized quite differently because of differences in strategy, environmental conditions, and technology.

3. *Environmental Conditions*: The key factor in the external environment that is relevant to organizing is uncertainty. Some enterprises face competitive environments that change rapidly and are quite complex, while others face relatively stable conditions. Generally, turbulent environments call for organizing decisions that lead to less formalization and centralization in the organizational structure.

4. *Technology*: The processes by which an enterprise transforms inputs into outputs may also affect organizing decisions. Some research suggests that organizing decisions that lead to high degrees of formalization, centralization, and work specialization are more appropriate for routine technologies and that the converse is true for non-routine technologies.

Importance of Organizing

1. Focus on, and facilitate the attaining of objectives.
2. Arrangement positions and jobs within the hierarchy.
3. Define responsibilities and line of authority of all levels.
4. Creating relationships that will minimize friction.

Basic Elements of Formal Organizations

1. *Centralization and Decentralization*: The level at which most decisions are made in the organization.

2. *Delegation of Authority*: The process of assigning work from top level to lower levels along with right to achieve the work.

   Factors determining degree of authority delegation:

   (a) Organization's size.
   (b) Importance of duty or decision.
   (c) Task complexity.
   (d) Organizational culture.
   (e) Qualities of subordinates.
3. *Span of Control (Supervision)*: Number of subordinates that can be adequately supervised by one supervisor.
4. *Division of Service*.
5. *Departmentation*: Group of activities into departments, divisions or other homogeneous units.

Motivation

Internal and external factors that stimulate desire and energy in people to be continually interested in and committed to a job, role, or subject, and to exert persistent effort in attaining a goal.

Significance of Motivation

- Higher efficiency in productivity.
- Low absenteeism and turnover.
- Facilitates change.
- Harmonious human relations.
- A better public image of the company.

Pecuniary Incentives: They are financial incentives which are paid directly or indirectly in money.

Non-pecuniary Incentives: They are non-financial incentives which provide psychological and emotional satisfaction.

- Challenging work.
- Recognition and status.
- Job security.
- Independence and responsibility.
- Healthy competition.
- Opportunity for growth.
- Participation of employees in management

Theories of Motivation

- Maslow's Need Priority Model
- Herzberg's Two-Factor Theory

- McGregor's Theory X and Theory Y
- Ouchi's Theory Z

Maslow's Need Priority Model

- Human needs form a particular structure or hierarchy.
- Lower level needs must be satisfied at least partially before the higher level need emerges.
- Various need levels are independent and overlapping.
- As soon as one need is satisfied, another need emerges.
- A satisfied need is not a motivator as it ceases to influence human behaviour.

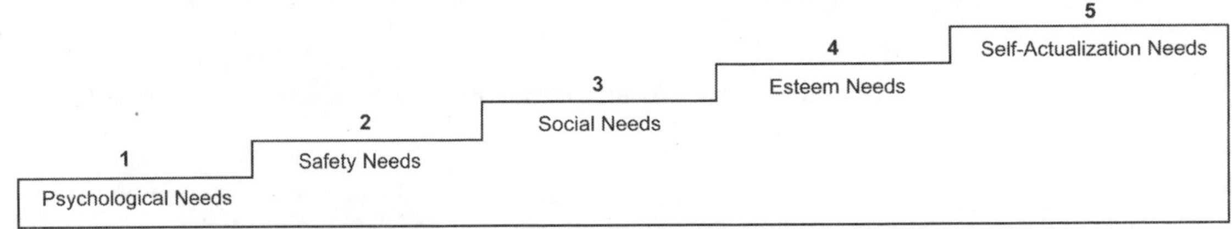

Critical Appraisal of Maslow's Need Priority Model

- Needs are not the only determinant of behaviours.
- The theory gives oversimplification of human needs and motivation.
- The hierarchy needs are not always fixed.
- The theory is based on relatively small sample.
- There is no definite evidence that a need is cease to influence a human behaviour once it is satisfied.

Herzberg's Two-Factor Theory

- Hygiene factors are necessary to maintain a reasonable level of satisfaction.
- Hygiene factors do not provide satisfaction to the employees; however their absence will dissatisfy them.
- These factors are related to the conditions under which the job is performed.

Hygiene Factors	Motivating Factors
Inter-personal relationship with peers	Achievement
Inter-personal relationship with supervisors	Recognition
Inter-personal relationship with subordinates	Advancement
Salary	Opportunity for growth
Job security	Independence and responsibility
Personal life	Work profile
Working condition	
Status	

Critical Appraisal of Herzberg's Two-Factor Model

- It is based on a small sample of 200 accountants and engineers which are not sufficient for the general workforce.
- It gives too much focus on satisfaction rather than performance level.
- The distinction between hygiene factors and motivating factors is not fixed.

McGregor's Theory X and Theory Y

They are created and developed by Douglas McGregor at the MIT Sloan School of Management in the 1960s that have been used in human resource management, organizational behaviour, and organizational development.

Theory X Assumptions: *Management's role is to pressurize and control employees.*

- People have an inherent dislike for work and will avoid it whenever possible.
- People must be coerced, controlled, directed, or threatened with punishment in order to get them to achieve the organizational objectives.
- People prefer to be directed, do not want responsibility, and have little or no ambition.
- People seek security above all else.

Theory Y Assumptions: *Management's role is to develop the potential in employees and help them to release that potential towards common goals.*

- Work is as natural as play and rest.
- People will exercise self-direction if they are committed to the objectives (they are not lazy).
- Commitment to objectives is a function of the rewards associated with their achievement.
- People learn to accept and seek responsibility.
- Creativity, ingenuity, and imagination are widely distributed among the population. People are capable of using these abilities to solve an organizational problem.
- People have potential.

Ouchi's Theory Z

Ouchi's Theory Z is often referred to as the "Japanese Management Style".

It advocates a combination of the best of Theory Y and modern Japanese management, placing a large amount of freedom and trust with workers, and assumes that workers have a strong loyalty and interest in team-working and the organization.

Characteristics of Theory Z

- Long-term employment and job security.
- Implicit, informal control with explicit, formalized measures.
- Slow evaluation and promotion.
- Moderately specialized careers.
- Concern for a total person, including their family.

Morale

In simple terms: *It is the capacity of a group of people to draw together steadily and consistently in pursuit of a common purpose.*

It is also known as esprit de corps, is a term used for the capacity of people to maintain belief in an institution or a specific goal.

Factors Influencing Morale within the Workplace

1. Job security.
2. Management style.
3. Staff feeling that their contribution is valued by their employer.
4. Realistic opportunities for merit-based promotion.
5. The perceived social or economic value of the work being done by the organization as a whole.
6. The perceived status of the work being done by the organization as a whole.
7. Team composition.
8. The work culture.

Leadership

In simple terms: *It is the art of motivating a group of people to act towards achieving a common goal.*

Leadership Style

- *Autocratic Leadership*: Where a leader exerts high levels of power over his or her employees.
- *Bureaucratic Leadership*: Bureaucratic leaders work "by the book", ensuring that their staff follow procedures exactly.
- *Charismatic Leadership*: The leader injects huge doses of enthusiasm into his or her team, and is very energetic in driving others forward.
- *Democratic Leadership/Participative Leadership*: Although a democratic leader will make the final decision, he or she invites other members of the team to contribute to the decision-making process.
- *Laissez-faire Leadership*: This French phrase means "leave it be" and is used to describe a leader who leaves his or her colleagues to get on with their work.
- *People-oriented Leadership/Relations-oriented Leadership*: The leader is totally focused on organizing, supporting and developing the people in the leader's team.
- *Servant Leadership*: A form of democratic leadership, as the whole team tends to be involved in decision-making.
- *Task-oriented Leadership*: A highly task-oriented leader focuses only on getting the job done, and can be quite autocratic.
- *Transactional Leadership*: The leader has the right to "punish" team members if their work does not meet the pre-determined standard.

- *Transformational Leadership*: A true leader who inspires his or her team with a shared vision of the future.

Situational Leadership

There is no one "right" way to lead or manage that suits all situations. One must consider the following before choosing the leadership style:

- The skill levels and experience of the members of the team.
- The work involved (routine or new and creative).
- The organizational environment (stable or radically changing, conservative or adventurous).
- Own preferred or natural style.

A good leader will switch instinctively between styles according to the people and work they are dealing with.

Managerial Control

Controlling is the measurement and correction of performance in order to make sure that enterprise objectives and the plans devised to attain them are accomplished.

—Harold Koontz

In simple terms: *Control consists of verifying whether everything occurs in conformity with the plan adopted, the instructions issued, and principles established.*

Characteristics of Control

- It is a continuous process.
- It is a management process.
- It is embedded in each level of organizational hierarchy.
- It is forward looking.
- It is closely linked with planning.
- It is a tool for achieving organizational activities.

The Elements of Control

The four basic elements in a control system:

1. The characteristic or condition to be controlled.
2. The sensor.
3. The comparator.
4. The activator.

Program Evaluation and Review Technique (PERT)

It is a method to analyze the tasks involved in completing a given project, especially the time needed to complete each task, and identifying the minimum time needed to complete the total project.

PERT Convention

- A PERT chart is a tool that facilitates decision-making.
- Two consecutive events in a PERT chart are linked by activities, which are conventionally represented as arrows.
- The events are presented in a logical sequence and no activity can commence until its immediately preceding event is completed.
- The planner decides which milestones should be PERT events and also decides their "proper" sequence.
- A PERT chart may have multiple pages with many sub-tasks.

Critical Path Method (CPM)

The essential technique for using CPM is to construct a model of the project that includes the following:

1. A list of all activities required to complete the project (also known as work breakdown structure).
2. The time (duration) that each activity will take to completion.
3. The dependencies between the activities.

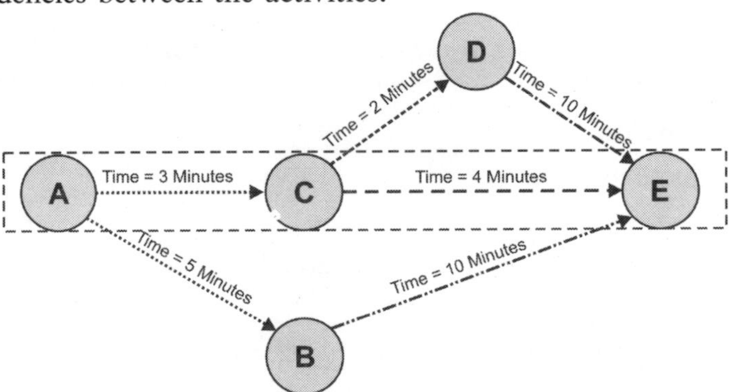

- There are five steps in the process starting from A and arriving at E
- ACE is the shortest path (Shortest duration of completing the process)

Business Communication

It is a kind of communication which is used to promote a product, service, or organization. Also used for relaying information within the business.

In simple terms: *The communication aimed at creating value for business.*

Internal	External
Corporate Vision	Branding
Strategies	Marketing
Plans	Advertising
Corporate Culture	Customer Relations
Shared Values and Guiding Principles	Public/Investor Relations
Employee Motivation	Media Relations
Cross-pollination of Ideas	Business Negotiations

Topics under Business Communication

- Marketing
- Branding
- Customer Relations
- Consumer Behaviour
- Advertising
- Public Relations
- Corporate Communication
- Community Engagement
- Research and Measurement
- Reputation Management
- Interpersonal Communication
- Employee Engagement
- Online communication
- Event management

Methods of Business Communication

1. *Web-based Communication*: With the advent of Internet and online services this medium has gained massive popularity.

2. *E-mails*: An instantaneous medium of written communication worldwide.

3. *Reports*: An important documenting activity of any department (sales reports, performance reports, annual reports, audit reports, progress reports, feasibility reports, white papers, etc).

4. *Presentations*: Very popular method of communication in all types of organizations, usually involving audio visual material, like copies of reports, or material prepared in Power Point or Adobe Flash.

5. *Telephonic Conference Meetings*: Allowing long distance speech.

6. *Forum Boards*: Allow people to instantly post information at a centralized location.

7. *Face to Face Meetings*: Personal interaction which should be succeeded by a written document about the interaction and follow up (minutes of the meeting).

Channels of Business Communication

1. Internet
2. Print Media (Publications)
3. Radio
4. Television
5. Ambient Media
6. Outdoor
7. Word of Mouth

E-MAIL COMMUNICATION DECORUM

Professional relationships are built on effective communication, respect and trust, which are earned when one demonstrates daily that the organization is worthy of supporters' investments of time, energy and money. Today most of the official letters are in the form of electronic data (e-mail).

E-mail is an extremely popular form of communication in both the business and personal communication landscapes, but it can often lead to major problems if the underlying tone of the e-mail message is misinterpreted at one end. If the parties involved are in different emotional states of mind, the slightest disagreement through e-mail can quickly spiral out of control leading to a full blown argument.

- *Target Recipients*: The most pertinent aspect of e-mail writing is to know the target recipients. All other things will depend on it. In professional organizations, the hierarchy makes a huge difference when it comes to e-mail communication.
- *Portrayal of the Recipients*: If you are reaching out to people who have already supported your organization, forge the relationship by declaring how important they are to your mission.
- *The Purpose of the Message to the Recipients*: Whether your goal is education, inspiration, registration or donation, make sure that recipients will know how you want them to take action.
- *Tone*: Friendly or professional? E-mail lends itself to a more conversational tone than quill and ink on crisp ivory letterhead, but be sure to represent your organization in the manner it deserves.
- *Authenticity of Information*: Make sure that the information is correct and appropriate. Also have a few other people to re-check them.
- *Spellings and Vocabulary*: Professional communications require attention to detail.
- *Ending the E-mail*: Whether the objective is education, inspiration, registration or donation, it must be made sure that recipients get to know how we want them to take action. Moreover, the ending must have a thanking note with a request to receive their reply.
- *The Opt-Out Clause*: One should always add an opt-out clause to the bottom of the message—even if the recipients have given the permission to e-mail them. By providing a simple, consistent means for enabling people to "unsubscribe" from your e-mail communications, you demonstrate your flexibility by acknowledging that constituent preferences can change.
- *Proofreading and Checking*: Check and cross check if the e-mail contains any spelling, grammatical or factual errors. Correct them as soon as they are detected.

Subject Line

Although some of the recipients may appreciate a clever opening, clear, concise language will certainly suffice. Be up front with supporters about the reason for the message—vagueness may cause recipients to mistake the note for unsolicited e-mail. We may even use the subject line to reiterate our call to action, particularly if we are sending a follow-up communication such as a pledge reminder or membership renewal.

Some Important Points to be Noted while Deciding a Subject Line

1. *Keep it Short and Simple*: Do not let the subject line run longer than 50 characters (6-7 words).

2. *Important Information First*: Make sure that the most important information is mentioned first so that the email becomes quite vivid.

3. *Personalization*: Use of recipient's name in the subject is effective in many some cases.

4. *Urgency*: Notification of urgency must be made only and only when the matter is really urgent.

Body Text

Here is where we can either find a shining pearl (useful information) in a sea shell (body text) or dead snail (useless story).

1. *Stick to the Point*: Do not make an e-mail longer than it needs to be. Reading an e-mail is harder than reading printed communications and a long e-mail can be a bit gloomy to read. We all know corporate people won't have extra business hours to devote on such e-mails; after all they are not paid to read never ending e-mails.

2. *Use Bullets*: Make use of numerical bullets to make points and facts. It can be use as a quick reference.

3. *Customize Accordingly*: Different hierarchy levels require different character of e-mails. For example, one can have a personal tone while communicating with peers and subordinates, but, the same cannot be followed when the e-mail is intended for bosses.

4. *Standardized Templates*: An easy way to save time and energy is to follow standard procedure. When in dearth time, use standardized templates of previous communications made.

5. *Do not Write in Capitals*: It makes a communication loud. People at all levels will feel the heat once they receive such e-mails. In many organizations, one may face disciplinary actions on following this procedure.

6. *Follow the Message Thread*: Always click on 'Reply' rather than 'New Mail' to maintain the chain of messages for the recipients to refer other mails if need be.

7. *Do not Overuse Reply to All*: Use 'Reply to All' if there is a need for the message to be seen by each person who received the original message.

8. *Avoid Abbreviations*: Do not use abbreviations such as BTW (by the way) and LOL (laugh out loud) in business communications. The recipient might not be aware of the meanings of the abbreviations and even they do not appear professional. At most, one can use FYI (For Your Information), only and only if it is prevalent in the organization.

9. *Avoid Forwarding Chain Mails*: Sometimes it blocks the server and one may fall into a trap of unprofessional activities within the organization. Let's remember that the IP Address can be tracked in a matter of seconds.

10. *Do not Ask to Recall a Message*: Chances are that your message has already been delivered and read. A recall request would appear stupid. It is better to send a fresh e-mail with

an apology and the information about the error committed in the previous mail. This will look much more honest and sensible than trying to recall a message.

11. *Use Active Instead of Passive*: For instance, 'we will update you by the end of the day, today', sounds better than 'The updation will be provided to you by the end of the day, today'. The first sounds more dependable, whereas the latter, especially when used frequently, sounds unnecessarily formal.

12. *Avoid using Urgent and Important*: Avoid them as much as possible in an e-mail body text or subject line. Make use of them if it is a really, really urgent or important message. An apt situation would be when particular information, if not available, would result in breakdown of a process.

13. *Keep Your Language Gender Neutral*: Avoid using racist language such as: 'The presenter should have **his** signature on the document'. Apart from using **he/she**, one can also use the neutral gender: 'The document should have the signature of the presenter'.

14. *Use CC: Field Scarcely*: Try not to use the cc: field unless the recipient in the cc: field knows why they are receiving a copy of the message. Using the cc: field can be confusing since the recipients might not know who is supposed to act on the message. Also, when responding to a cc: message, should you include the other recipient in the cc: field as well? This will depend on the situation. In general, do not include the person in the cc: field unless you have a particular reason for wanting this person to see your response. Again, make sure that this person will know why they are receiving a copy.

15. *Always the E-mail Policy of the Organization*: The policy includes all the do's and don'ts concerning the use of the company's e-mail system and should be distributed amongst all employees. Secondly, get trained by company veterans to fully understand the importance of e-mail etiquette.

Professional E-mail Characteristics

There are numerous varieties of e-mails that one encounters while working in the corporate world. Every e-mail has a different character. Care must be taken to deal with each e-mail accordingly.

Whatever be the character of an e-mail there is one thing that must be followed throughout, "Always reply by giving Respect". The one thing which is not acceptable from professionals in the corporate world is "Emotional Response" or "Emotions attached with Response".

When replying an official e-mail, leave the following outside the company doors:

- Anger
- Frustration
- Ego
- Excitement

The only solution is to be Rational.

Think Analyze, Evaluate and Design a reply which looks professional. A professional reply is the one which hold business interest and possible alternate solutions, as the case may be.

One may come across the following categories of e-mails:

1. Request Mails
2. Information Seeking Mails
3. Work Allocation Mails
4. Urgent Action Mails
5. Escalation Mails
6. Stinker Mails
7. Appreciation Mails
8. Promotion/Demotion Mails
9. Organizational Announcement Mails
10. Department-Wise Information Mails
11. Policy Mails

Marketing

The activity, set of institutions, and processes for creating, communicating, delivering, and exchanging offerings that have value for customers, clients, partners, and society at large.

—American Marketing Association

FOUR Ps of Marketing Mix

1. *Product*: It deals with the specifications of the actual goods or services, and how it relates to the end-user's needs and wants.

2. *Pricing*: This refers to the process of setting a price for a product, which need not be monetary; it can simply be what is exchanged for the product or services, like time, energy or attention.

3. *Placement (or Distribution or Place)*: It refers to the channel by which a product or service is made available to the customer, for example, point-of-sale placement or retailing.

4. *Promotion*: This includes advertising, sales promotion, publicity, and personal selling, branding and various methods of promoting the product, brand, or company.

Services Marketing Calls upon Extra Three Ps

1. *People*: Any person coming into contact with customers can have an impact on overall satisfaction. As a result of this, they must be appropriately trained, well-motivated and the right type of person.

2. *Process*: It involves providing a service and the behaviour of people, which can be crucial to customer satisfaction.

3. *Physical Evidence*: It is often vital to offer potential customers the chance to see what a service would be like. This is done by providing physical evidence such as case studies, testimonials or demonstrations.

Branding

In simple terms: *Creating reference of certain products or services in mind.*

A brand is a name, term, design, symbol, or other feature that distinguishes products and services from competitive offerings. A brand represents the consumers' experience with an organization, product, or service.

Advertising

It is a paid form of public presentation and promotion of ideas in an expressive manner which is aimed at masses.

- The manufacturer may determine what goes into advertisement.
- Pervasive and impersonal medium.

Objectives of Advertising

- Maintain demand for well-known goods.
- Introduce new and unknown goods.
- Increase demand for well-known goods/products/services.
- Create awareness.

Requirements of a Good Advertisement

- Attract attention
- Provide awareness
- Stimulate interest
- Create a desire
- Bring about action

Eight Steps in an Advertising Campaign

- Market research
- Setting aims and objectives
- Budgeting
- Choice of media (television, print media, radio, web, outdoor, etc.)
- Design and wording
- Co-ordination
- Test results

Personal sales

It is an oral presentation given by a salesperson that approaches individuals or a group of potential customers.

- Live, interactive relationship
- Personal interest
- Attention and response
- Interesting presentation

Sales Promotion

It a technique of using short-term incentives to encourage buying of products.

- Instant appeal
- Anxiety to sell

Examples: Coupons or a sale.

Drawbacks of Sales Promotion

- May not build customer loyalty or encourage future repeat buys.
- It is easily copied by competition.
- It cannot be used as a sustainable source of differentiation.

Consumer Behaviour

It is the process and activities people engage in when searching for, selecting, purchasing, using, evaluating, and disposing of products and services so as to satisfy their needs and desires.

—*Belch and Belch*

In simple terms: *Consumer behaviour is the study of when, why, how, where and what consumer(s) will or will not buy.*

The 'Black Box' Model *(Black Box = Consumer's Mind)*

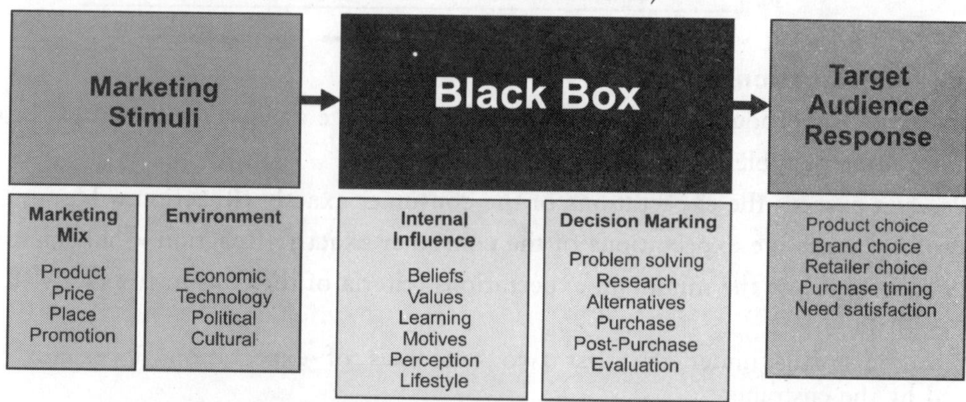

Importance of Studying Consumer Behaviour

- To implement the marketing concept.
- To plan for influencing buyer-seller exchanges to meet organizational goals.
- To understand complex influences on consumption processes.
- To increase confidence in predictions regarding consumer responses to the marketing strategy.
- To avoid self presumptions.

Consumer's Information Sources

- Personal sources: Family members, friends, relatives, colleagues, etc.
- Commercial sources: Product promotion by shop owners, dealers, etc.
- Public sources: Audio visual media, print media.

Information Evaluation

The consumers compare the brands and products that are in their minds. Consumers evaluate alternatives in terms of the functional and psychological benefits that they can get from the product oɪ services.

Consumer's Decision Process

Consumers try to simplify decision making by reducing the amount of information processing.

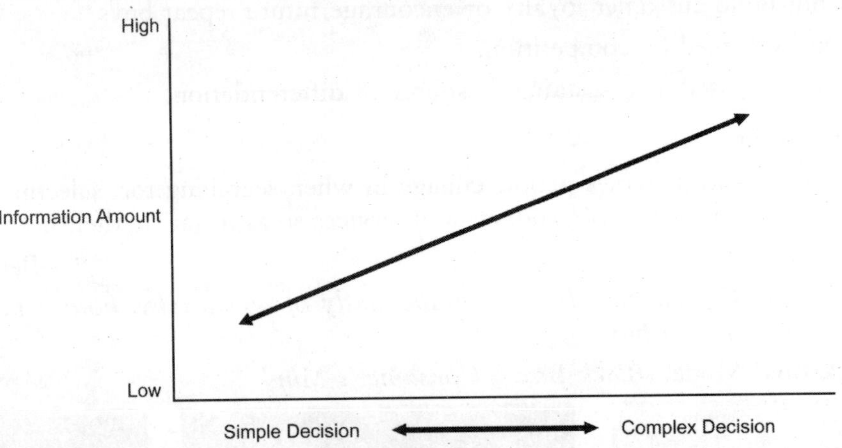

Post-purchase Evaluation

As consumers use products, they evaluate its performance against their own expectations. There are three possible outcomes of these evaluations:

1. Product exceeds the expectations of the consumer exactly (Reaction = Happy).
2. Product meets the expectations of the consumer exactly (Reaction = Satisfactory).
3. Product is below the minimum expectations criteria of the consumer exactly (Reaction = Unhappy).

When product falls under the first two outcomes of expectation, it usually will be repurchased by the customer.

Introduction to Statistics

5

Statistics

It is the collection, organization, presentation, analysis and interpretation of numerical data.

It is applicable to a wide range of academic disciplines, from the natural and social sciences to the humanities, government and business.

Elements of Statistics

- Data Collection
- Data Analysis
- Experimental Design
- Survey Sampling
- Observational Study
- Descriptive Statistics
- Statistical Inference
  - ✔ *Estimation*
  - ✔ *Testing Hypothesis*

Types of Statistics

- *Descriptive:* Summarize or describe a collection of data.
- *Inferential:* Used for drawing inferences about a process or population being studied.
- *Mathematical:* Concerned with the theoretical basis of the subject.
- *Exact:* Based on exact probability statements.

Statistical Methods

1. Experimental and Observational Studies
2. Levels of Measurement
3. Statistical Techniques

Experimental and Observational Studies

A common goal for a statistical research project is to investigate causality, and in particular to draw a conclusion on the effect of changes in the values of predictors or independent variables on dependent variables or response.

Levels of Measurement

There are four types of measurement which have different degrees of usefulness in statistical research.

- ✔ Nominal
- ✔ Ordinal
- ✔ Interval
- ✔ Ratio

Statistical Techniques (Some well known)

- ✔ Analysis of Variance (ANOVA)
- ✔ Chi-Square Test
- ✔ Correlation
- ✔ Factor Analysis
- ✔ Mann-Whitney U
- ✔ Mean Square Weighted Deviation (MSWD)
- ✔ Person Product-Moment Correlation Coefficient
- ✔ Regression Analysis
- ✔ Spearman's Rank Correlation Coefficient
- ✔ Student's t-Test
- ✔ Time Series Analysis

Limitations of Statistics

- ✔ It is not suitable to the study of qualitative phenomenon.
- ✔ It does not study individual measurement.
- ✔ Statistical laws are not exact.
- ✔ Statistical table may be misused if it is based on incomplete information.

Classification of Data

In simple terms: Categorization of data for its most effective and efficient use as per specific requirements.

1. *Natural Breaks Classification*: It is a manual data classification method that divides data into classes based on the natural groups in the data distribution.
2. *Quantile Classification*: This method classifies data into a certain number of categories with an equal number of units in each category.
3. *Equal Interval Classification*: This method sets the value ranges in each category equal in size.
4. *Standard Deviation Classification*: It finds the mean value, and then places class breaks above and below the mean at intervals of either 0.25, 0.5 or, one standard deviation until all the data values are contained within the classes.

Frequency Distribution

In simple terms: *Statistical data arranged to show the frequency with which the possible values of a variable occur.*

1. *Tabular Representation of Data*
    - Simple frequency distribution (or it can be just called a frequency distribution).
    - Cumulative frequency distribution.
    - Grouped frequency distribution.
    - Cumulative grouped frequency distribution.
2. *Graphical Representation of Data*
    - Bar Graph.
    - Histogram.
    - Frequency Polygon.
    - Scatter Diagram.
3. *Numerical Representation of Data*: We can use a single number to represent many numbers. We will discuss three types of numerical representation of data in chapters 5, 6, and 8.
    - Measures of Central Tendency.
    - Measures of Variability.
    - Measures of Association.

Illustration: Simple Frequency Distribution

Data Set - High Temperatures for 30 Days				
50	45	49	50	43
49	50	49	45	49
47	47	44	51	51
44	47	46	50	44
51	49	43	43	49
45	46	45	51	46

To Create a Frequency Distribution from this Data We Proceed as Follows:

1. Identify the highest and lowest values in the data set. Highest temperature is **51** and the lowest temperature is **43.**

2. Create a column with the title '**Temperature**'. Enter the highest score at the top, and include all values within the range from the highest score to the lowest score.

3. Create a tally column to keep track of the scores as you enter them into the frequency distribution. Once the frequency distribution is completed you can omit this column. Most printed frequency distributions do not retain the tally column in their final form.

4. Create a frequency column, with the frequency of each value, as show in the tally column, recorded.

5. At the bottom of the frequency column record the total frequency for the distribution proceeded by N =.

6. Enter the name of the frequency distribution at the top of the table.

Temperature	Tally	Frequency
51	////	4
50	////	4
49	~~////~~ /	6
48		0
47	///	3
46	///	3
45	////	4
44	///	3
43	///	3
	N	**30**

Illustration: Cumulative Frequency Distribution

Data Set - High Temperatures for 30 Days				
50	45	49	50	43
49	50	49	45	49
47	47	44	51	51
44	47	46	50	44
51	49	43	43	49
45	46	45	51	46

To Create a Cumulative Frequency Distribution We Proceed as Follows:

1. Create a frequency distribution.
2. Add a column entitled cumulative frequency.
3. The cumulative frequency for each score is the frequency up to and including the frequency for that score.
4. The highest cumulative frequency should equal N (the total of the frequency column).

Temperature	Tally	Frequency	Cumulative Frequency
	////	4	30
51			
50	////	4	26
49	~~////~~ /	6	22
48		0	16
47	///	3	16
46	///	3	13
45	////	4	10
44	///	3	6
43	///	3	3
	N	**30**	

Illustration: Grouped Frequency Distribution

Data Set - High Temperatures for 50 Days				
57	39	52	52	43
50	53	42	58	55
58	50	53	50	49
45	49	51	44	54
49	57	55	59	45
50	45	51	54	58
53	49	52	51	41
52	40	44	49	45
43	47	47	43	51
55	55	46	54	41

To Create a Grouped Frequency Distribution We can Follow as per the Following Steps:

1. Select an interval size to have 7-20 class intervals.
2. Create a class interval column and list each of the class intervals (here its = 2).
3. Each interval must be the same size, they must not overlap, there may be no gaps within the range of class intervals.
4. Create a tally column (it is optional).
5. Create a mid-point column for interval mid-points.
6. Create a frequency column.
7. Enter N = some value at the bottom of the frequency column.

Class Interval	Tally	Interval Mid-point	Frequency
57-59	~~////~~ /	58	6
54-56	~~////~~ //	55	7
51-53	~~////~~ ~~////~~ /	52	11
48-50	~~////~~ ////	49	9
45-47	~~////~~ //	46	7
42-44	~~////~~ /	43	6
39-41	////	40	4
		N	**50**

Illustration: Grouped Cumulative Frequency Distribution

Class Interval	Tally	Interval Mid-point	Frequency	Cumulative Frequency
57-59	~~||||~~ /	58	6	50
54-56	~~||||~~ //	55	7	44
51-53	~~||||~~ ~~||||~~ /	52	11	37
48-50	~~||||~~ ////	49	9	26
45-47	~~||||~~ //	46	7	17
42-44	~~||||~~ /	43	6	10
39-41	////	40	4	4
		N	**50**	

To Create a Grouped Cumulative Frequency Distribution We Proceed as Follows:

1. Create a frequency distribution.
2. Add a column entitled Cumulative Frequency.
3. The cumulative frequency for each score is the frequency up to and including the frequency for that score.
4. The highest cumulative frequency should equal N (the total of the frequency column).

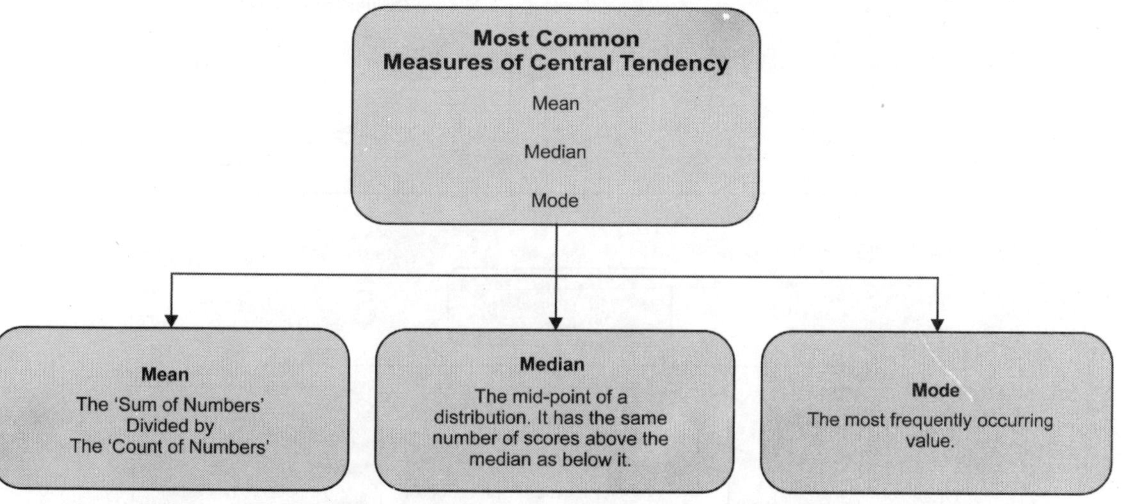

Illustration: Simple Average, Median and Mode

Number of Men	Apples Collected	Central Tendency
1	22	
1	21	
1	20	**Mean** = 203/11 = 19.13
1	23	
1	19	**Median** = 11/2 = 5th Item = 20
1	18	
1	18	**Mode** = Most Repeated = 18
1	12	
8	**153**	

Illustration: Weighted Average

$$\text{Weighted Mean} = \frac{\text{Sum of (Weight (W)} \times \text{Numbers (X))}}{\text{Sum of Weights}}$$

Wages Per Day (X)	Number of Workers (W)	WX	Weighted Average
20	20	400	
16	15	240	$\frac{\text{Sum of (Weight} \times \text{Numbers)}}{\text{Sum of Weights}}$
6	5	30	
Total	**40**	**670**	**16.75**

Relationship between Mean, Median and Mode

- When the value of mean, median and mode are equal, it is symmetrical distribution.
- When the value of mean, median and mode is not equal, it is asymmetrical or skewed distribution.

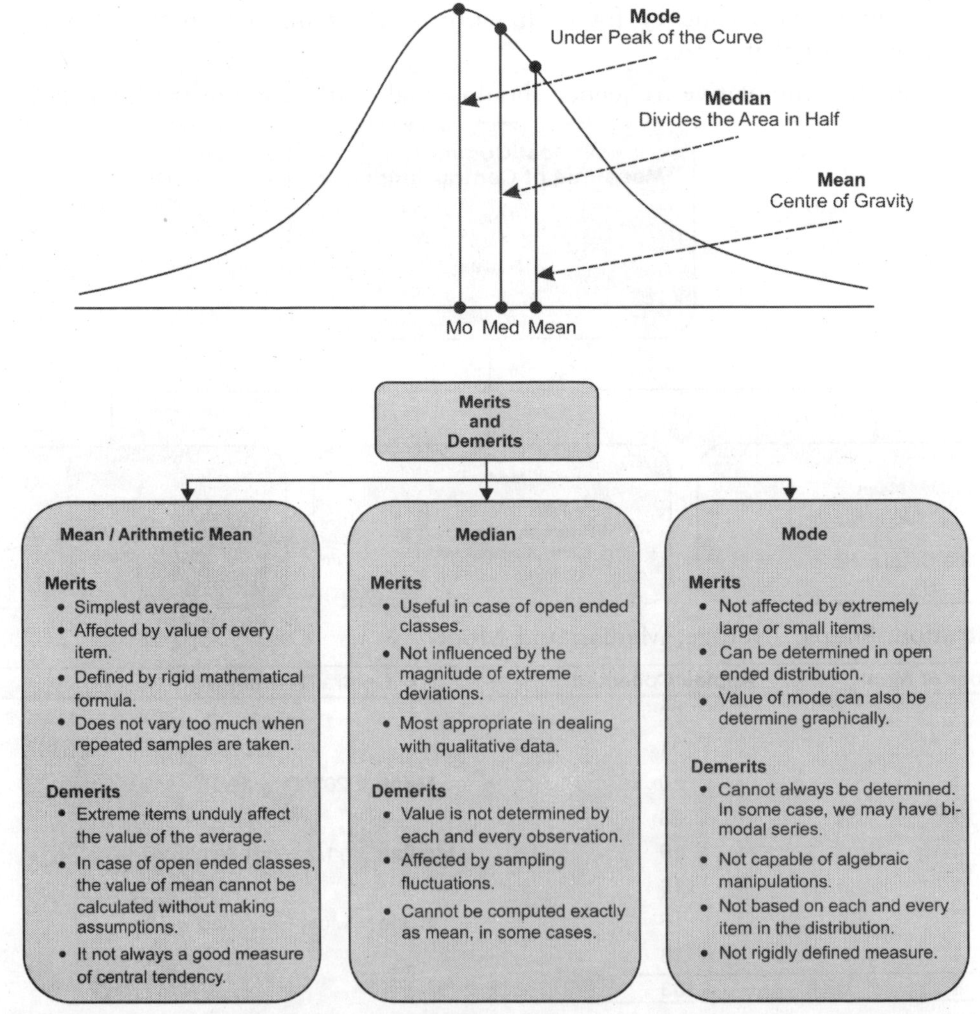

Geometric Mean

In simple terms: *It is the Nth root of the product of N items or values.*

Geometric Mean = $((X_1)(X_2)(X_3)........(X_N))^{1/N}$

where

- X = Individual score
- N = Sample size (Number of scores)

Illustration: Find the Geometric Mean of 1, 2, 3, 4 and 5.

- Step 1: N = 5, the total number of values. Find 1/N.
  1/N = 0.2
- Step 2: Now find Geometric Mean using the formula.
  [(1) × (2) × (3) × (4) × (5)] × 0.2 = (120) × 0.2
  So, Geometric Mean = 2.60517

Harmonic Mean

In simple terms: *It is the reciprocal of the arithmetic mean of the reciprocals of a specified set of numbers.*

Harmonic Mean = $N / (1/X_1+1/X_2+1/X_3+1/X_4+.......+1/X_N)$

where

- X = Individual score
- N = Sample size (Number of scores)

Illustration: Find the Harmonic Mean of 1, 2, 3, 4 and 5.

- Step 1: Calculate the total number of values.
  N = 5
- Step 2: Now find Harmonic Mean using the above formula.
  = 5/(1/1 + 1/2 + 1/3 + 1/4 + 1/5)
  = 5/(1 + 0.5 + 0.33 + 0.25 + 0.2) = 5/2.28
  So, Harmonic Mean = 2.19

Which Average to Use?

Mean	Median	Mode	Geometric Mean	Harmonic Mean
All cases apart from Median, Mode, Geometric and Harmonic Mean	Open-Ended Grouped Distribution	Qualitative Analysis	Averaging Ratios & Percentages	Comparison of variable values with constant quantities of another variable

Measures of Dispersion

In simple terms: *It is the measure of variation of the items from the average value.*

Significance

- To determine the reliability of an average.
- To serve as the basis for the control of the variability.

- To compare two or more series with regard to their variability.
- To facilitate the use of other statistical measures.

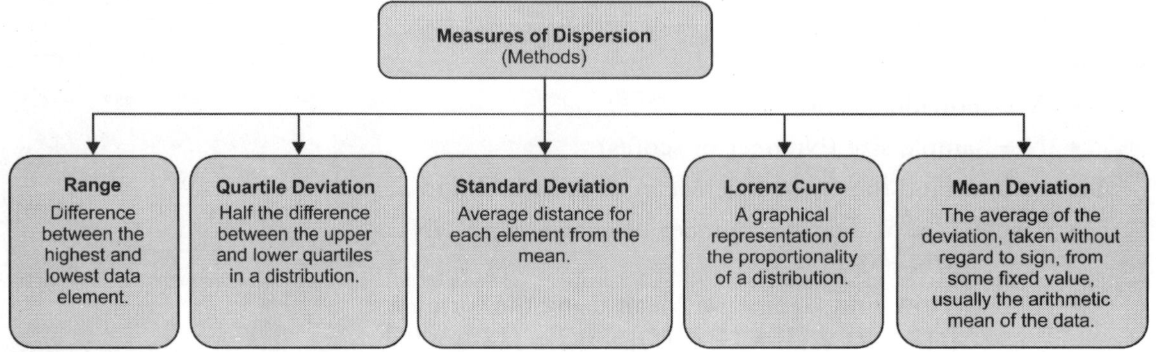

1. Range

Largest item – Smallest item

2. Coefficient of Range

Largest item – Smallest Item / Largest Item + Smallest Item

3. Quartile Deviation

Third Quartile – First Quartile / 2

$$Q_1 = \frac{N+1}{4}$$

$$Q_2 = 3\left(\frac{N+1}{4}\right)$$

4. Coefficient of Quartile Deviation

Third Quartile – First Quartile / Third Quartile + First Quartile

5. Simple Illustration: Quartile Deviation and Coefficient of Quartile Deviation

Student	Marks in Ascending Order
English	12
Accounts	**15**
Math	20
Economics	28
Human Resource	30
Business Studies	**40**
Statistics	50
Sum of X	**195**

Number (N) = 7

$$Q_1 \ \frac{7+1}{4} = 2$$

$$Q_3 \ \frac{3\times(N+1)}{4} = 6$$

Quartile Deviation $\dfrac{Q_3 - Q_1}{2} = \dfrac{40 - 15}{2} = 12.5$

Coefficient of QD $\dfrac{Q_3 - Q_1}{Q_3 + Q_1} = \dfrac{40 - 15}{40 + 15} = 0.455$

6. Standard Deviation

$$\sigma = \sqrt{\frac{\Sigma(X - \text{Mean})^2}{N}}$$

Simple Illustration

Student	(Marks) X	X - Mean	(X - Mean)^2
English	2	–3	9
Accounts	4	–1	1
Math	4	–1	1
Economics	4	–1	1
Human Resource	5	0	0
Business Studies	5	0	0
Statistics	7	2	4
Law	9	4	16
Sum of X	**40**		**32**
N =	8		
Mean =	$\frac{40}{8} = 5$		

Standard Deviation = $\sqrt{\dfrac{32}{8}} = 2$

The mean and the standard deviation of a set of data are usually reported together. In a certain sense, the standard deviation is a "natural" measure of statistical dispersion if the center of the data is measured about the mean.

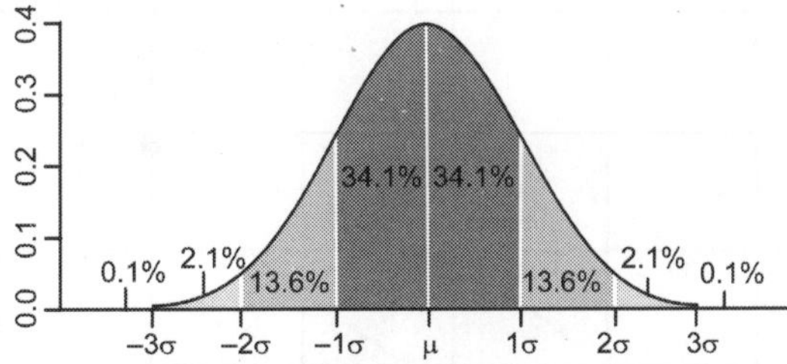

For the normal distribution, less than one standard deviation accounts for 68.27 per cent of the set; while the other two standard deviations account for 95.45 per cent; three standard deviations account for 99.73 per cent; and four standard deviations account for 99.994 per cent.

7. Lorenz Curve

It was developed by Max O. Lorenz in 1905 for representing income distribution.

Characteristics of Lorenz Curve

- It always starts at (0, 0) and ends at (1, 1).

- The Lorenz curve is not defined if the mean of the probability distribution is zero or infinite.
- The Lorenz curve for a probability distribution is a continuous function.
- If the variable being measured cannot take negative values, the Lorenz curve:
  (a) Cannot rise above the line of perfect equality,
  (b) Cannot sink below the line of perfect inequality,
  (c) Is increasing, and
  (d) Is a convex function.
- If the variable being measured can take negative values but has a positive mean, then the Lorenz curve will sink below the line of perfect inequality and is a convex function.
- If the variable being measured can take negative values and has a negative mean, then the Lorenz curve will be above the line of perfect equality, except at the end points, and is a concave function.

Simple Illustration

Share of Aggregate Income, US Households
(by the way, income by household is different from income by family)

Year	Lowest 20%	Next Lowest 20%	Middle 20%	Second Highest 20%	Highest 20%
1979	4.2	11.1	17.5	24.4	42.8

Cumulative Fraction of Aggregate Income, US Households, 1979 (in percentage)

	Lowest 20%	Next Lowest 20%	Middle 20%	Second Highest 20%	Highest 20%
Income %	0.042	0.111	0.175	0.244	0.428
Cumulative Income %	0.042	0.153	0.328	0.572	1

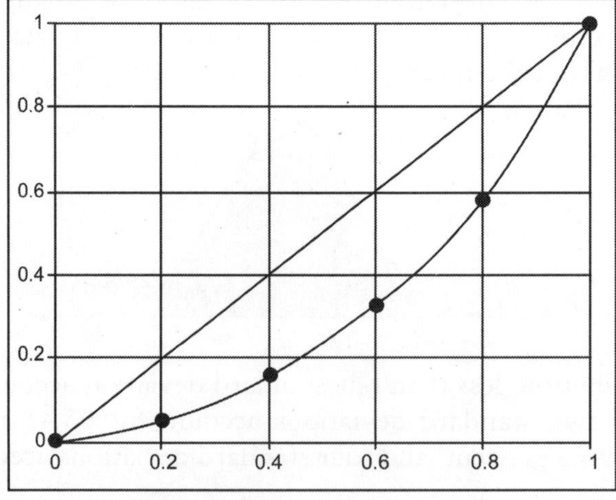

8. Mean Deviation

$$\frac{\sum|X - \text{Mean}|}{N}$$

The two parallel lines within which we have the difference of x and mean denotes 'Modulas' or 'Absolute Value'. It simply means 'ignoring signs'.

Simple Illustration

Student	(Marks) X	X - Mean	(X - Mean)²
English	92	2	2
Accounts	75	–15	15
Math	95	5	5
Economics	90	0	0
Human Resource	98	8	8
Sum of X	**450**		**30**
	N = 5		

$$\text{Mean} = \frac{450}{2} = 90 \qquad \text{Mean Deviation} = \frac{30}{5} = 6$$

Conclusion: *This means that on an average the student's test scores deviated by 6 points from the mean.*

Which Measure of Dispersion to Use?

Type of Distribution	Purpose of Investigation
Avoid Standard Deviation	**Use any of the three (Range, Quartile Deviation or Mean Deviation)**
If there are few numbers or contains extreme values	In case of elementary treatment
Avoid Mean Deviation	**Use Standard Deviation**
If the frequency is generally skewed	In case of future statistical analysis
Avoid Quartile Deviation	
If there are gaps around quartiles	
For open ended classes Quartile Deviation is preferred	

Skewness

It refers to lack of symmetry in the shape of a frequency distribution.

—Morris Hamburg

$$\text{Skewness} = \frac{E(x-\mu)^3}{\sigma^3}$$

where μ is the mean of x, σ is the standard deviation of x, and E represents the expected value of a particular quantity.

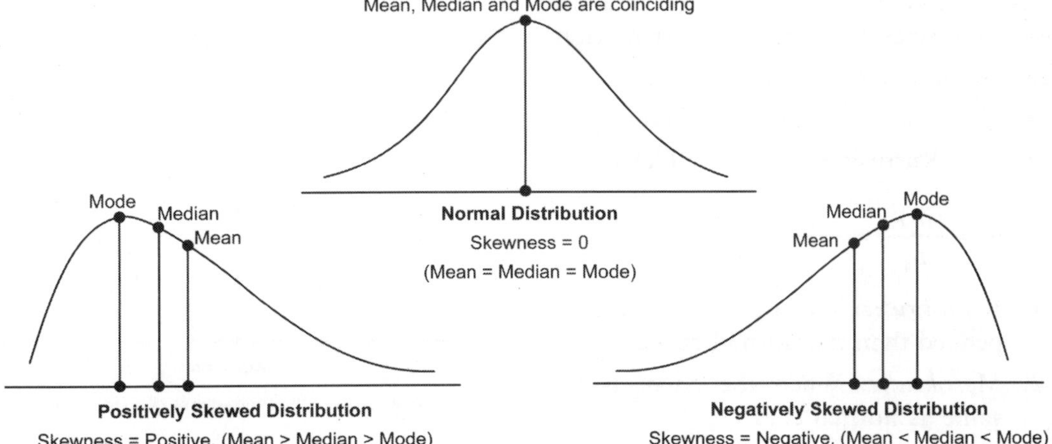

Normal Distribution
Skewness = 0
(Mean = Median = Mode)

Positively Skewed Distribution
Skewness = Positive, (Mean > Median > Mode)

Negatively Skewed Distribution
Skewness = Negative, (Mean < Median < Mode)

$$\text{Karl Pearson's Coefficient of Skewness} = \frac{\text{Mean} - \text{Mode}}{\text{Standard Deviation}}$$ Relationship: Mode = 3Median – 2 Mean

$$\text{Bowley's Coefficient of Skewness} = \frac{Q_3 + Q_1 - 2}{Q_3 - Q_1}$$

Test of Skewness

1. Value of mean, median and mode do not coincide.
2. Quartiles are not equidistant from the median.
3. Frequencies are not equally distributed.
4. Data when plotted on graph does not give normal bell-shaped curve.

Moments

It is the expected value of a positive integral power of a random variable.

The first moment is the mean of the distribution.

Moments about Mean

$$\mu_1 = \frac{\Sigma(X - \text{Mean})}{N} = 0 \qquad \mu_2 = \frac{\Sigma(X - \text{Mean})^2}{N}$$

$$\mu_4 = \frac{\Sigma(X - \text{Mean})^3}{N} = 0 \qquad \mu_3 = \frac{\Sigma(X - \text{Mean})^4}{N}$$

Moments about Arbitrary Origin

$$\mu_1 = \frac{\Sigma(X - A)}{N} = 0 \qquad \mu_2 = \frac{\Sigma(X - A)^2}{N}$$

$$\mu_4 = \frac{\Sigma(X - A)^3}{N} = 0 \qquad \mu_3 = \frac{\Sigma(X - A)^4}{N}$$

Kurtosis

It is a measure of whether the data are peaked or flat relative to a normal distribution.

Kurtosis in Greek means 'bulginess'.

- High Kurtosis = High Peaked Curve
- Low Kurtosis = Relatively Flat Curve

$$K = \frac{(\mu_2)^2}{\mu_4} = \frac{(\text{2nd Moment})^2}{\text{4th Moment}}$$

1. *Leptokrutic*: When the curve is more peaked than the normal curve.
2. *Mesokrutic*: When the curve is the same as normal curve.
3. *Platykrutic*: When the curve is more flat topped than the normal curve.

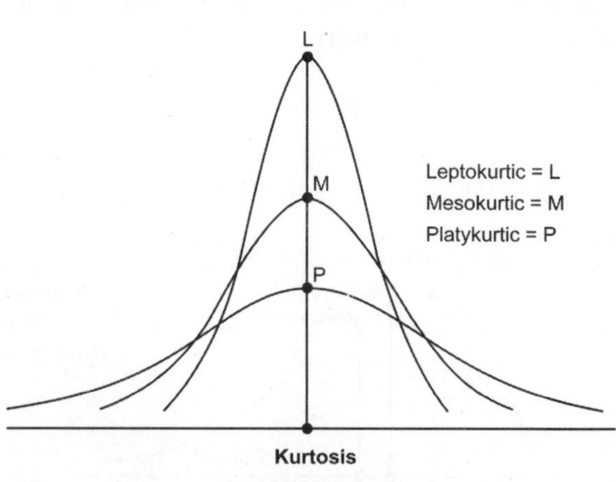

Kurtosis

A Measure of the Peakedness of a Distribution

Correlation Analysis

It attempts to determine the 'degree of relationship' between variables.

—*Ya Lun Chou*

Correlation and Causation

- Correlation may be due to chance particularly when the data pertain to a small sample.
- It is possible that both the variables are influenced by one or more other variables.
- It may be that case, where both the variables may be influencing each other—we cannot say which the cause is and which the effect is.

Types of Correlation

1. Positive and Negative
2. Linear and Non-linear
3. Simple, Partial and Multiple.

Significance of Studying Correlation

- Helpful in understanding economics behaviour: Analyzing relationship between demand, supply, price, income and expenditure.
- Strives to reduce uncertainty.
- Aids in locating critical variables.

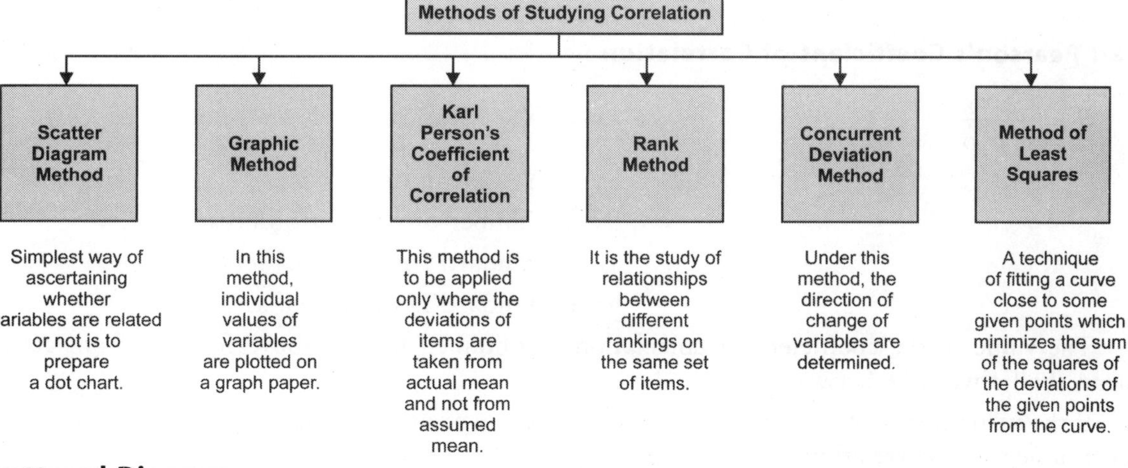

Scattered Diagram

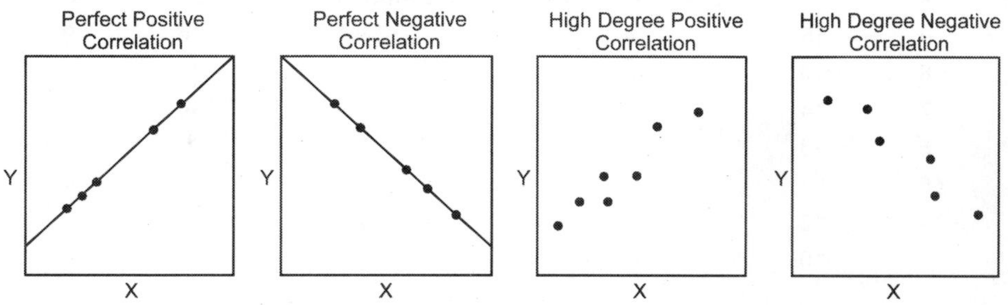

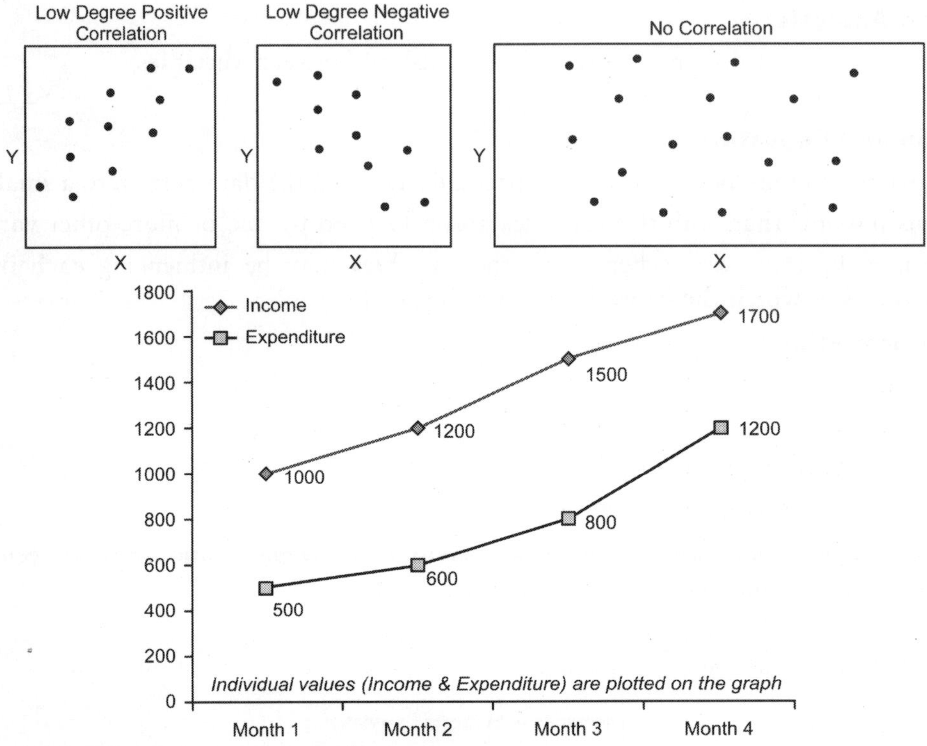

Karl Pearson's Coefficient of Correlation

$$R = \frac{\Sigma xy}{N\sigma_x\sigma_y}$$

x = (X – Mean of X)

y = (Y – Mean of Y)

N = Number of pairs of observation

σ_x = Standard Deviation of series X

σ_y = Standard Deviation of series Y

The value of the coefficient of correlation as obtained by the above formula from actual mean shall always be between $\pm$ 1.

If the value is in +, it would mean the correlation is positive and if the value is in –, it would mean a negative correlation.

Description	X	Y	x (X – Mean of X)	y (Y – Mean of Y)	x^2	y^2	xy
	9	15	4	3	16	9	12
	8	16	3	4	9	16	12
	7	14	2	2	4	4	4
	6	13	1	1	1	1	1
	5	11	0	–1	0	1	0
	4	12	–1	0	1	0	0
	3	10	–2	–2	4	4	4

Contd.

	2	8	–3	–4	9	16	12
	1	9	–4	–3	16	9	12
ΣX	45	108	0	0	60	60	57
N	9	9					
Mean	5	12					

$$\text{Covariance } \frac{\Sigma xy}{N} = \frac{57}{9} = 6$$

$$\sigma_x \sqrt{\frac{\Sigma x^2}{N}} = \frac{7.75}{3} = 2.58$$

$$\sigma_y \sqrt{\frac{\Sigma y^2}{N}} = \frac{7.75}{3} = 2.58$$

$$\text{Coefficient of } \sqrt{\frac{\Sigma xy}{N\sigma_x\sigma_y}} = \frac{57}{9 \times (2.58 \times 2.58)} = 0.95$$

Rank Method

$$R = 1 - \frac{6\Sigma D^2}{N^3 - N}$$

D = Difference of ranks between paired items

N = Number of pairs of observation

R = Rank of Coefficients

Description	R1	R2	D (R1 – R2)	D2
	1	3	-2	4
	2	2	0	0
	3	1	2	4
ΣX	6	6	0	8
N	3	3		

$$\text{Coefficient of Correlation } 1 - \frac{6\Sigma D^2}{N^3 - N} = 1 - \frac{6 \times 8}{27 - 3}$$

$$= 1 - \frac{48}{24} = -1$$

Concurrent Deviation Method

$$R_c = \pm \sqrt{\pm\left(\frac{2c - n}{n}\right)}$$

c = Number of concurrent deviations

n = Number of pairs of observation compared

Year	Supply	D_x	Price	D_y	D_xD_y (Number of Positive Signs)
1985	160		292		
1986	164	+	280	–	–
1987	172	+	260	–	–
1988	182	+	234	–	–

Contd.

1989	166	–	266	+	–
1990	170	+	254	–	–
1991	178	+	230	–	–
1992	192	+	190	–	–
1993	186	–	200	+	–
					C = 0

According to the Formula $R_c = \sqrt{\frac{2 \times 0 - 8}{8}} = -1$

Method of Least Squares

Most widely used in practice, it helps in fitting a trend line to the data in such a manner that the following two conditions are satisfied:

1. $\Sigma(Y - Y_c) = 0$
2. $\Sigma(Y - Y_c)^2 =$ Least

The line obtained by this method is known as 'the line of best fit'.

Straight line trend equation is $Y_c = a + bX$

- Y_c = Trend values.
- a = Intercept of computed trend figure of Y variable when $X = 0$.
- b = Slope of the trend line/amount of change in Y variable associated with change in one unit of X variable.

In order to determine the value of 'a' and 'b', the following equations are to be solved:

$\Sigma Y = Na + b\Sigma X$ (It is merely the summation of the given function)

$\Sigma XY = a\Sigma X + b\Sigma X^2$ (It is the summation of X multiplied by the given function)

After getting the values of 'a' and 'b' we will have the complete equation of the line of best fit.

Regression Analysis

It attempts to establish the 'nature of relationship' between variables.

—*Ya Lun Chou*

In simple terms: *It attempts to establish the functional relationship between variables thereby providing a mechanism for prediction, or forecasting.*

Strengths of Regression Analysis

- Regression analysis provides an opportunity to specify hypotheses concerning the nature of effects (action theory), as well as explanatory factors.
- When it is successfully executed (with a statistically valid adjustment), regression analysis can produce a quantitative estimate of net effects.

Limitations of Regression Analysis

- The technique is demanding because it requires quantitative data relating to several thousand individuals.
- Implementing the data collection can be time-consuming and expensive.

- Regression analysis is likely to reach the conclusion that there is a strong link between two variables, whereas the influence of other, more important, variables may not have been estimated.
- Relations between the different explained and explanatory variables are often circular (*X* explains *Y* and *Y* explains *X*). Here, the method is inapplicable.
- The observations must present sufficiently contrasted evolutions to allow for adjustment.

Usage of Regression Analysis

1. Prediction
2. Variable selection
3. Model specification (system explanation)
4. Parameter estimation

Regression Models

1. Linear Regression Model
   - Simple Linear
   - Multiple Linear
2. Non-Linear Regression Model

Difference between Correlation and Regression

Correlation	Regression
It is the degree of co-variability between two variables (X and Y).	It studies the nature of relationship between variables.
It is not sure if one variable is dependent on another.	One variable is taken as dependent and the other as independent.
There may be a nonsense correlation between two variables.	There is nothing like nonsense regression.
It is dependent on change of scale and origin.	They are independent of change or origin but not of scale.

Regression Lines

The most typical type of regression is linear regression (meaning one can use the equation for a straight line, rather than some other type of curve).

It is constructed using the least-squares method (the line you choose is the one that minimizes the sum of the squares of the distances between the line and the data points).

It's customary to use "*a*" or "alpha" for the intercept of the line, and "*b*" or "beta" for the slope; so linear regression gives you a formula of the form: $Y_c = a + bX$

where

- *a* and *b* are constants (also called parameters of the line)
- Parameter *a* determines the intercepts, i.e. what will be the value of *Y* if *X* is zero.
- Parameter *b* determines the slope.

If we take the case of X and Y, we shall have two regression lines as the regression of X on Y and the regression of Y on X.

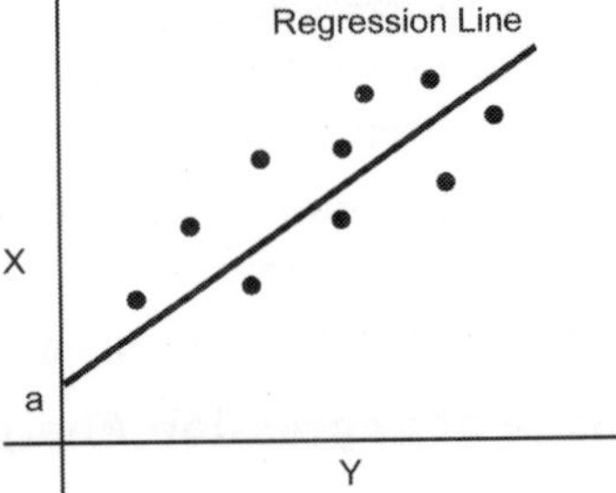

- The regression lines of Y on X gives the most probable values of Y for a given value of X.
- The regression lines of X on Y gives the most probable values of X for a given value of Y.
- When there is either perfect positive or perfect negative correlation the line will coincide.
- The farther the two lines from each other the lesser the degree of correlation.
- Regression lines cut each other at the point of average of X and Y.

Simple Illustration

Description	Father (X)	Son (Y)	X^2	Y^2	XY
Observation 1	6	9	36	81	54
Observation 2	2	11	4	121	22
Observation 3	10	5	100	25	50
Observation 4	4	8	16	64	32
Observation 5	8	7	64	49	56
Sum S	**30**	**40**	**220**	**340**	**214**

Here **N = 5** Observations

Regression of *Y* on *X*

$\Sigma Y = Na + b\Sigma X$: $40 = 5a + b30$ ...(i)

$\Sigma XY = a\Sigma X + b\Sigma X^2$: $214 = 30a + b220$ ...(ii)

To find the value of *a* and *b*, lets multiply equation (i) with such a number that can bring either *a* or *b* value equal to equation (ii).

Here, we see that $5a$ and $b30$ have a common multiple 6. So, let us multiply equation (i) by 6 to bring the value of *a* equal to equation (ii).

$240 = 30a + 180b$.................... (i) After multiplying by 6

$214 = 30a + 220b$.................... (ii) Same as above

On subtracting equation (ii) from equation (i) we get the following:

$$26 = -40b$$

Hence, $b = -0.65$

We get the value of $a = 11.9$, by placing the value of *b* in equation (i).

Regression Equation of Y on X is $Y = 11.9 - 0.65X$

Regression of *X* on *Y*

$\Sigma X = Na + b\Sigma Y$: $30 = 5a + b40$ ...(iii)

$\Sigma XY = a\Sigma Y + b\Sigma Y^2$: $214 = 40a + b340$ ...(iv)

To find the value of *a* and *b*, lets multiply equation (i) with such *a* number that can bring either *a* or *b* value equal to equation (ii).

Here, we see that 5*a* and *b*40 have a common multiple 8. So, let's multiply equation (i) by 6 to bring the value of *a* equal to equation (ii).

$$240 = 40a + b320 \ldots\ldots\ldots\ldots\ldots\ldots \text{(iii) After multiplying by 6}$$
$$214 = 40a + b340 \ldots\ldots\ldots\ldots\ldots\ldots \text{(iv) Same as above}$$

On subtracting equation (iv) from equation (iii) we get the following:

$$26 = -20b$$

Hence, $b = -1.3$

We get the value of $a = 16.4$, by placing the value of b in equation (i).

Regression Equation of X on Y is $X = 16.4 - 1.3Y$

Index Numbers

In simple terms: *They are devices of measuring the differences in the magnitude of a group of related variables.*

Uses of Index Numbers	Characteristics	Problems in Index Numbers
Helps in framing suitable policies.	They are specialized averages.	Selection of a base period.
They reveal trend and tendencies.	They measure the net change in the group of related variables.	Selection of number of items.
	They measure the effect of change over a period of time.	Obtaining price quotations.
		Choice of average.
		Selection of appropriate weights.
		Selection of appropriate formula.

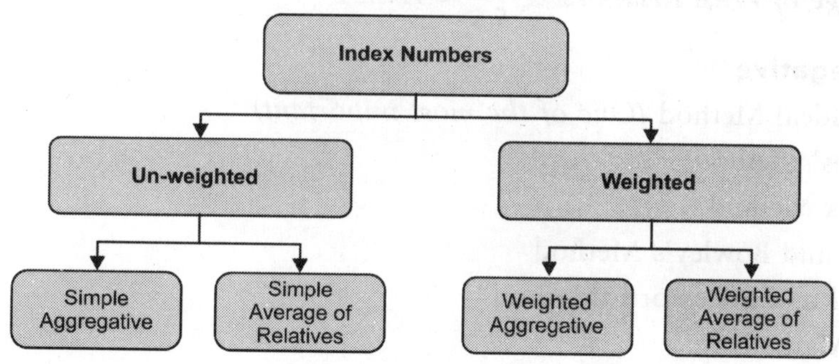

Simple Aggregative

$$P_{01} = \frac{\Sigma p_1}{\Sigma p_0} \times 100$$

Σp_0 = Sum of Current Year Prices of Various Commodities

Σp_1 = Sum of Base Year Prices of Various Commodities

Simple Average of Price Relatives

$$P_{01} = \frac{\sum \frac{p_1}{p_0} \times 100}{N}$$

where

p_0 = Current Year Prices of Various Commodities

p_1 = Base Year Prices of Various Commodities

N = Number of Items

Simple Illustration

Commodity	Price in 1980 (Base p_0)	Price in 1985 (Base p_1)	Price of Relatives (p_1/p_0) x 100
A	50	70	140.0
B	40	60	150.0
C	80	90	112.5
D	110	120	109.1
E	20	20	100.0
Σ	**300**	**360**	**611.6**

N = 5

Simple Aggregative $\frac{360}{300} = 120$. This means that as compared to the base year, there is a net increase in the prices of commodities included in the index to the extent of 20 per cent.

Simple Average of Price Relatives $\frac{611.6}{5} = 122.32$

Weighted Aggregative

- Fisher's Ideal Method *(One of the most important)*
- Laspeyres' Method
- Paasche's Method
- Dorbish and Bowley's Method
- Marshall and Edgeworth Method
- Kelly's Method

Laspeyres' Method

$$P_{01} = \frac{\sum p_1 q_0}{\sum p_1 q_0} \times 100$$

Paasche's Method

$$P_{01} = \frac{\sum p_1 q_1}{\sum p_0 q_1} \times 100$$

Dorbish and Bowley's Method

$$P_{01} = \frac{\left\{\frac{\sum p_1 q_0}{\sum p_1 q_0} \times \frac{\sum p_1 q_1}{\sum p_0 q_1}\right\} \times 100}{2}$$

Fisher's Ideal Method

$$P_{01} = \sqrt{\frac{\sum p_1 q_0}{\sum p_0 q_0} \times \frac{\sum p_1 q_1}{\sum p_0 q_1}} \times 100$$

Marshall and Edgeworth Method

$$P_{01} = \frac{\sum (p_0 + q_1) \times p_1}{\sum (p_0 + q_1) \times p_0} \times 100$$

Kelly's Method *(SPV / SV, where P = p_1/p_0 x 100... and V = $p_0 q_0$)*

$$P_{01} = \frac{\sum p_1 q}{\sum p_0 q} \times 100$$

where

p_0 = Base Year Price
q_0 = Base Year Weights
p_1 = Current Year Price
q_1 = Current Year Weights
q = Average Weights of two or more years

Simple Illustration

Commodity	Year 1987		Year 1988		p_0q_0	p_1q_1	p_1q_0	p_0q_1
	Price (p_0)	Quantity (q_0)	Price (p_1)	Quantity (q_1)				
A	2	8	4	6	16	24	32	12
B	5	10	6	5	50	30	60	25
C	4	14	5	10	56	50	70	40
D	2	19	2	13	38	26	38	26
Sum Σ					**160**	**130**	**200**	**103**

N = 4

$$\text{Laspeyres's Method} = \frac{200}{160} \times 100 = 125.00$$

$$\text{Paasche's Method} = \frac{130}{103} \times 100 = 126.21$$

$$\text{Bowley's Method} = \frac{1.25 + 1.262}{2} \times 100 = 125.60$$

$$\text{Fisher's Method} = \sqrt{\frac{200 \times 130}{160 \times 103}} \times 100 = 125.60$$

$$\text{Marshall's Method} = \frac{200 + 130}{160 + 103} \times 100 = 125.50$$

Consumer Index

In simple terms: *It is a measure of the average price of consumer goods and services purchased by households.*

Methods for Constructing Consumer Index

1. *Aggregate Expenditure Method (Same as Laspeyres's Method)*

$$C_{01} = \frac{\sum p_1 q_0}{\sum p_0 q_0} \times 100$$

2. *Family Budget Method (SPV / SV, where $P = p_1/p_0 \times 100$... and $V = p_0 q_0$)*

$$C_{01} = \frac{\sum p_1 q_0}{\sum p_0 q_0} \times 100$$

Hence, we arrive at the same formula as above.

Time Series

In simple terms: *A time series is a set of statistical observations arranged in chronological order.*

Utility of Time Series

- Helps in understanding the past behaviour.
- Helps in planning future operations.
- Facilitating comparisons.
- Help in evaluating current accomplishments.

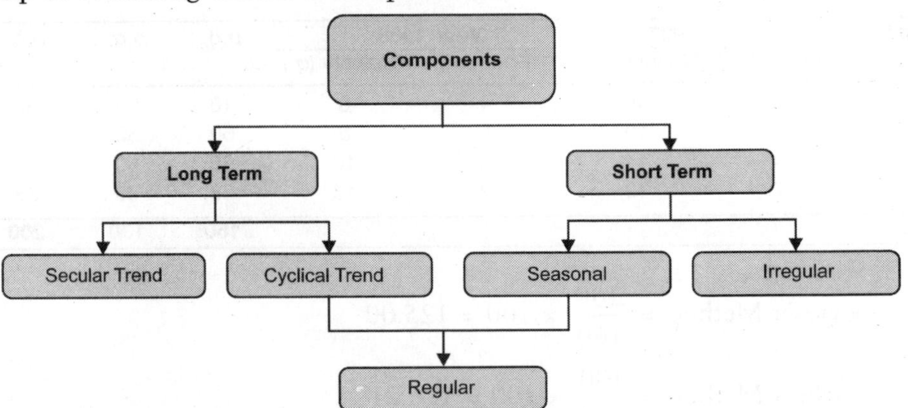

1. In time series analysis, it is an assumption that there is a multiplicative relationship between these four components.

- Symbolically, $Y = T \times S \times C \times I$

where Y denotes the product of the four elements; T = Trend; S = Seasonal component; C = Cyclical components and I = Irregular component. In the multiplicative model, it is assumed that the four components are due to different causes but they are not necessarily independent and they can affect one another.

2. Another approach is to treat each observation of a time series is the sum of these four components.

- Symbolically, $Y = T + S + C + I$

The additive model assumes that all the components of the time series are independent of one another.

Secular Trend

It is a long-term movement in time series. The general tendency of the time series is to increase or decrease or stagnate during a long period of time, which is called the secular trend or simply trend.

Methods of Measuring Trend

- Graphical method
- Method of semi-averages
- Method of moving averages
- Method of least squares

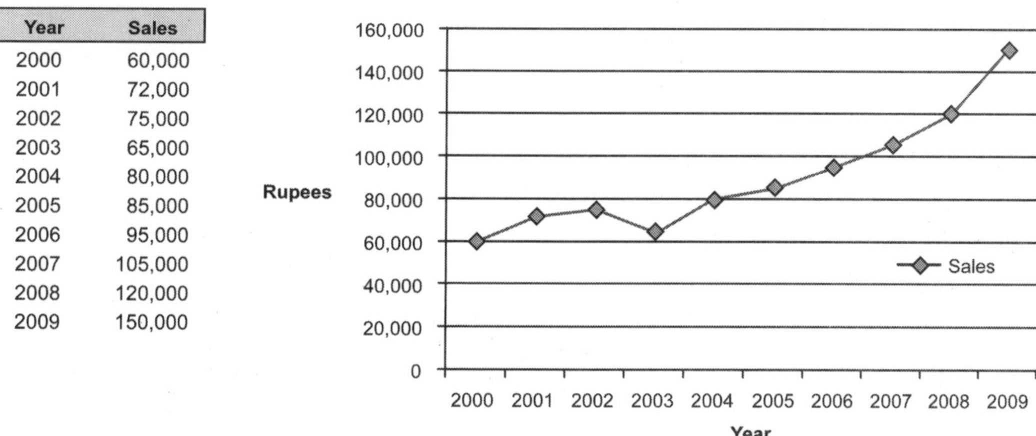

Year	Sales
2000	60,000
2001	72,000
2002	75,000
2003	65,000
2004	80,000
2005	85,000
2006	95,000
2007	105,000
2008	120,000
2009	150,000

Merits

- It is the simplest and easiest method. It saves time and labour.
- It can be used to describe all kinds of trends.
- This can be used widely in application.
- It helps to understand the character of time series and to select appropriate trend.

Demerits

- It is highly subjective. Different trend curves will be obtained by different persons for the same set of data.
- It is dangerous to use freehand trend for forecasting purposes.
- It does not enable us to measure trend in precise quantitative terms.

Method of Semi-averages

In this method, the given data is divided into two parts, preferably with the same number of years and then an average of each part is obtained. Thus, we get two points.

Year	Sales	Semi Total	Semi-Average	Trend Values
1991	60			59
1992	75	216	72	72
1993	81			85
1994	110			98
1995	106	333	111	111
1996	117			124

Difference in middle periods = 1995 – 1992 = 3 years

Difference in semi-averages = 111 – 72 = 39

Annual increase in trend = 39/3 = 13

Trend of 1991 = Trend of 1992 – 13........... 72 – 13 = 59

Trend of 1993 = Trend of 1992 + 13......... 72 + 13 = 85

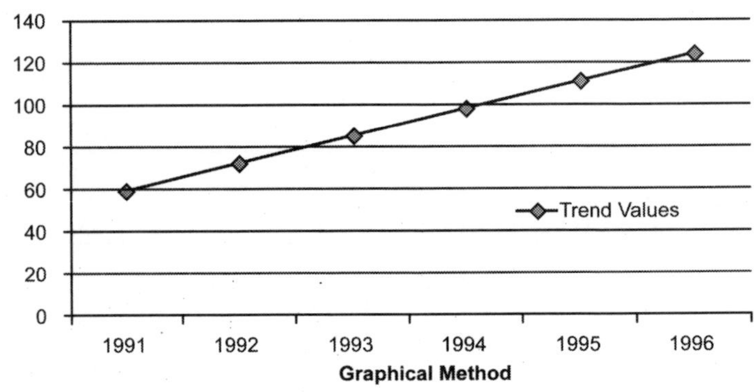

Graphical Method

Merits

- It is simple and easy to calculate.
- By this method every one getting same trend line.
- Since the line can be extended in both ways, we can find the later and earlier estimates.

Demerits

- This method assumes the presence of linear trend to the values of time series which may not exist.
- The trend values and the predicted values obtained by this method are not very reliable.

Method of Moving Averages

This method is very simple. It is based on arithmetic mean. These means are calculated from overlapping groups of successive time series data.

Year	Sales	3 Year Moving Total	3 Year Moving Average
1975	50		Trend Values
1976	36	129	43.0
1977	43	124	41.3
1978	45	127	42.3
1979	39	122	40.7
1980	38	110	36.7
1981	33	113	37.7
1982	42	116	38.7
1983	41	117	39.0
1984	34		

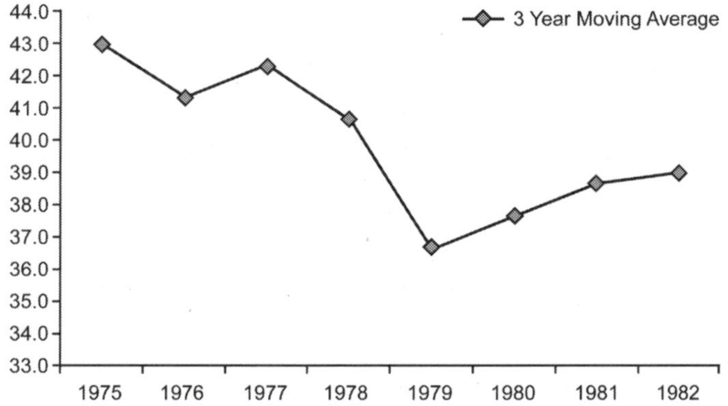

Merits

- The method is simple to understand and easy to adopt as compared to other methods.
- It is very flexible in the sense that the additions of a few more figures to the data, the entire calculations are not changed. We only get some more trend values.
- Regular cyclical variations can be completely eliminated by a period of moving average equal to the period of cycles.
- It is particularly effective if the trend of a series is very irregular.

Demerits

- It cannot be used for forecasting or predicting future trend, which is the main objective of trend analysis.
- The choice of the period of moving average is sometimes subjective.
- Moving averages are generally affected by extreme values of items.
- It cannot eliminate irregular variations completely.

Method of Least Squares

This method is widely used. It plays an important role in finding the trend values of economic and business time series. It helps for forecasting and predicting the future values. The trend line by this method is called the line of best fit.

The equation of the trend line is $y = a + bx$, where the constants a and b are to be estimated so as to minimize the sum of the squares of the difference betweens the given values of y and the estimate values of y by using the equation. The constants can be obtained by solving two normal equations.

$$\Sigma Y = Na + b\Sigma X \quad (1)$$

$$\Sigma XY = a\Sigma X + b\Sigma X^2 \quad (2)$$

Here x represents time point and y are observed values. n is the number of pair-values.

Merits

- Since it is a mathematical method, it is not subjective so it eliminates personal bias of the investigator.
- By this method we can estimate the future values as well as intermediate values of the time series.
- By this method we can find all the trend values.

Demerits

- It is a difficult method. Addition of new observations makes recalculations.
- Assumption of straight line may sometimes be misleading since economics and business time series are not linear.
- It ignores cyclical, seasonal and irregular fluctuations.
- The trend can estimate only for immediate future and not for distant future.

Seasonal Variations

Seasonal variations are fluctuations within a year during the season. The factors that cause seasonal variation are:

- Climate and weather condition.
- Customs and traditional habits.

Methods for Measuring Seasonal Variations

- Method of simple averages.
- Ratio to trend method.
- Ratio to moving average method.
- Link relative method.

Cyclical Variations

They are recurrent variations in time series that extend over longer period of time, usually two or more years. Most of the time series relating to economic and business show some kind of cyclic variation.

A business cycle consists of the recurrence of the up and down movement of business activity. It is a four-phase cycle, namely:

- Prosperity
- Decline
- Depression
- Recovery

Irregular Variation

Irregular variations are also called erratic. These variations are not regular and which do not repeat in a definite pattern. These variations are caused by war, earthquakes, strikes flood, revolution, etc. This variation is short-term one, but it affect all the components of series.

Probability

It is the likelihood that a particular event will happen in the future.

Probability can be expressed as a fraction, ratio, or percentage.

Probability Theory is the branch of mathematics concerned with analysis of random phenomena.

$$P(E) = \frac{\text{Number of Outcomes Favorable to the Event}}{\text{Total Number of Possible Outcomes}}$$

Sample Point is the outcome of a random experiment.

Sample Space is the set of all possible outcomes, discrete and continuous.

Event is an outcome, thus a subset of sample space.

Probability Outcome is a number which ranges from zero to one.

- Zero: for an event which cannot occur.
- One: for an event which is certain to occur.

If the collection of all possible outcomes is U and the collection of desired outcomes is A, then the probability of the desired outcomes will be $P = A/U$.

Now, since A is a subset of U, the probability of the desired outcomes is $0 < P(A) < 1$, as discussed above.

If we throw a fair dice, any one of the six numbers 1, 2, 3, 4, 5 and 6 may come up. There are altogether 6 possible outcomes and the occurrence of each of these outcomes is equally likely. Hence, we conclude that each number has an equal chance to appear and the probability of throwing, say; the number 5 is equal to 1/6.

It is denoted as $P(5) = 1/6$.

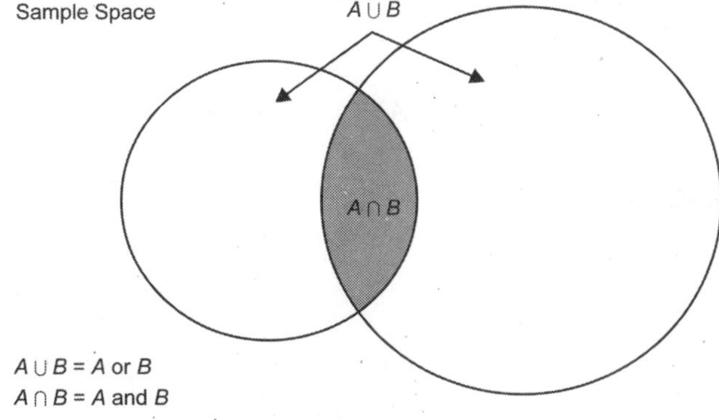

Uses of Probability	Theorems of Probability	
It is useful in making predictions about future.	**Addition Theorem**	If 2 events A and B are mutually exclusive then $P = (A \text{ or } B) = P(A) + P(B)$.
Helpful in managerial decisions in planning and controlling.	**Multiplication Theorem**	If 2 events A and B are mutually exclusive then $P = (A \text{ and } B) = P(A) \times P(B)$.
Helps in identifying the level of uncertainty.		

Discrete Probability Theory deals with events that occur in countable sample spaces.

Examples: Throwing dice and experiments with decks of cards, etc.

Continuous Probability Theory deals with events that occur in a continuous sample space.

Example: The random variable of birth weight.

Conditional Probability

In simple terms: *It is the probability that an event will occur, given that one or more other events have occurred.*

If two events A and B are dependent, then the conditional probability of B given A is:

$$P\ (B/A) = \frac{P(A \cap B)}{P(A)} = \frac{P(AB)}{P(A)}$$

If two events A and B are dependent, then the conditional probability of A given B is:

$$P\ (A/B) = \frac{P(A \cap B)}{P(B)} = \frac{P(AB)}{P(B)}$$

General rule of multiplication, if two events A and B are dependent, in terms of conditional probability will be:

$$P\ (A \text{ and } B) = P(B) \times \frac{P(A)}{P(B)}$$

$$P\ (A \text{ and } B) = P(A) \times \frac{P(B)}{P(A)}$$

If three events A, B and C are dependent, then the general rule of multiplication in terms of conditional probability will be:

$$P\ (ABC) = P(A) \times \frac{P(B)}{P(A)} \times \frac{P(C)}{P(AB)}$$

Permutation and Combination

Permutation: *An ordered arrangement of n different objects.*

Formula

$$P\ (N, R) = \frac{N!}{(N-R)!}$$

where

- N is the number of elements available for selection.
- R is the number of elements to be selected ($0 \le R \le N$).

Question: *Suppose three travelers arrive at a town where there are five hotels. In how many ways can they select room at different hotels?*

Answer

- Number of hotels available (N) = 5
- First traveler has 5 choices
- Second traveler has 4 choices
- Third traveler has 3 choices

Hence

$$P\,(5,\,3) = \frac{5!}{(5-3)!} = \frac{5\times4\times3\times2\times1}{2!}$$

$$= \frac{5\times4\times3\times2\times1}{2\times1} = 5 \times 4 \times 3 = 60$$

Simple Illustration

Find the permutations of the letters in the word STATISTICS

- Number of letters available (N) = 10
- Number of the letter S = 3
- Number of the letter T = 3
- Number of the letter A = 1
- Number of the letter I = 2
- Number of the letter C = 1

$$P = \frac{10!}{3!\times3!\times2!\times1!} = \frac{10\times9\times8\times7\times6\times5\times4\times3\times2\times1}{3\times2\times1\times3\times2\times1\times2\times1\times1\times1} = 50,400$$

Combination: *An unordered selection of r objects from a set of n (? r) different objects.*

Formula

$$^{N}C_{R} = \frac{N!}{R!\times(N-R)!}$$

Simple Illustration

In how many ways can a committee of four persons be chosen out of 10?

- Number of letters available (N) = 10
- Number of persons to be chosen = 4

$$^{10}C_{4} = \frac{10!}{4!\times(10-4)!} = \frac{10\times9\times8\times7\times6\times5\times4\times3\times2\times1}{4\times3\times2\times1\times6\times5\times4\times3\times2\times1} = 210$$

Theoretical Distribution

Empirical distributions: Distributions of scores that come from observation.

Theoretical distributions: It is based on mathematical formulas and logic. It is used in statistics to determine the probabilities. When empirical and theoretical distributions correspond, we can use the theoretical one to determine probabilities of an outcome, which will lead to inferential statistics. The main point to retain is that theoretical distributions represent the "best estimate" of how events would actually occur. As with all estimates, a theoretical distribution may produce predictions that vary from observation, but will produce good estimates.

Types of Theoretical Distributions

1. *Binomial Distribution*: Distribution of the frequency of events that can have only two possible outcomes.

2. *Rectangular Distribution (or Uniform Distribution)*: Distribution in which all possible scores have the same probability of occurrence.

3. *The Normal Distribution*: A theoretical frequency distribution for a set of variable data, usually represented by a bell-shaped curve symmetrical about the mean.

- It is a bell-shaped, theoretical distribution that predicts the frequency of occurrence of chance events.
- It is asymptotic: Its line continually approaches but never reaches a specified limit.
- The curve is symmetrical: Half of the total area is to the left, half to the right.
- The total area under the theoretical distribution is always 1. Because it is so, there is a correspondence between area and probability.

Binomial Probability Distribution

Consider a situation where there are only two possible outcomes (a "Bernoulli trial").

Example

- *Flipping a coin: The outcome is either a head or tail.*
- *Rolling a dice: For example, 6 or not 6 (i.e. 1, 2, 3, 4, 5)*

A binomial experiment is one that possesses the following properties:

1. The experiment consists of n repeated trials.
2. Each trial results in an outcome that may be classified as a success or a failure (hence the name, binomial).
3. The probability of a success, denoted by p, remains constant from trial to trial and repeated trials are independent.

Formula for the random variable X in binomial distribution is:

$$P(X) = C_x^n \, p^x q^{n-x}$$

where

n = the number of trials

x = 0, 1, 2... n

p = the probability of success in a single trial

q = the probability of failure in a single trial (i.e. $q = 1 - p$)

C_x^n is a combination

Poisson Probability Distribution

It is a widely used discrete probability distribution which was developed by the French mathematician Simeon Denis Poisson in 1837.

The Poisson random variable satisfies the following conditions:

1. The number of successes in two disjoint time intervals is independent.

2. The probability of a success during a small time interval is proportional to the entire length of the time interval.

The probability distribution of a Poisson random variable X representing the number of successes occurring in a given time interval or a specified region of space is given by the formula:

$$P(X) = \frac{e^{-\mu}\mu^{-x}}{x!}$$

where

$x = 0, 1, 2, 3...$

$e = 2.71828$ (but use your calculator's e button)

μ = mean number of successes in the given time interval or region of space.

The Z score

In simple terms: *A statistical measure that quantifies the distance (measured in standard deviations) a data point is from the mean of a data set.*

Z scores are a special application of the transformation rules. The z score for an item, indicates how far and in what direction, that item deviates from its distribution's mean, expressed in units of its distribution's standard deviation. The mathematics of the z score transformation are such that if every item in a distribution is converted to its z score, the transformed scores will necessarily have a mean of zero and a standard deviation of one.

Z scores are sometimes called "standard scores". The z score transformation is especially useful when seeking to compare the relative standings of items from distributions with different means and/or different standard deviations.

Z scores are especially informative when the distribution to which they refer, is normal. In every normal distribution, the distance between the mean and a given z score cuts off a fixed proportion of the total area under the curve. Statisticians have provided us with tables indicating the value of these proportions for each possible z score.

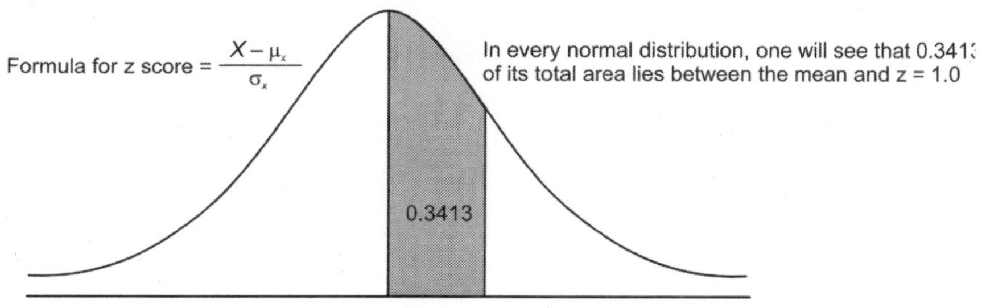

References

Reference for Statistics

- Statistical Methods by S.P. Gupta and M.P. Gupta (Sultan Chand & Sons)
- Wikipedia
- mnstate.edu/wasson/ed602lesson3.htm
- easycalculation.com/statistics
- moneychimp.com
- textbooksonline.tn.nic.in
- tutors4you.com
- *answers.com*

Reference for Business Management

The references (via intensive web search and hand books) are drawn with an aim to get simplest definitions and explanations on varied concepts. Some important sites and books are as under:

- Introduction-to-Management
- http://www.telelavoro.rassegna.it/fad/socorg03/l4/Elton%20Mayo-Hawthorne.htm
- MBA – My Note
- South Western
- Management Concepts and Practices by C.B. Gupta: Sultan Chand & Sons

Reference for Human Resource

- T.N. Chhabra (Dhantpat Rai & Co.)
- WikiAnswers,
- Hiroshi Imai (JICA Expert)
- Presentation by Charlie Cook The University of West Alabama
- Businessdictionary.com
- skagitwatershed.org
- basiccollegeaccounting.com
- agniwesh.com
- dictionary.bnet.com

- performance-appraisal.com
- indianmba.com
- smallbusinessnotes.com
- humanresources.about.com

References for Economics

- S.K. Mishra and V.K. Puri by Himalaya Publication House
- Web Search: Investopedia, Wikipedia, Encyclopedia Britannica, Answers.com, Economic Expert, Economic Web Institute

References for Accounts

- T.S. Grewal, *Double Entry Book Keeping*, Sultan Chand and Sons
- investorwords.com
- Wikipedia.com
- answers.com
- streetauthority.com